Some Praise for

the
Journey

"There is no sentimental drivel here. With simplicity and charm, Herrington takes the real, everyday, seemingly commonplace experiences of life that most would overlook and turns them into word pictures that exemplify timeless truths - truths that we have become all too familiar with - and often ignored. Herein are stories that are amusing and encouraging - even convicting perhaps - to the Christian believer. *The Journey* puts some much needed "feet" to what we may already know and have long since believed in, and reminds us of what true Christian living is all about."

—Melvin Manickavasagam is a graduate of Reformed Theological Seminary and the truest of friends

the Journey

Thomas Herrington

the
Journey

Applying Spiritual
Truths to
Everyday Life

Tate Publishing & Enterprises

Published by Tate Publishing & Enterprises, LLC
127 E. Trade Center Terrace | Mustang, Oklahoma 73064 USA
1.888.361.9473 | www.tatepublishing.com

Tate Publishing is committed to excellence in the publishing industry. The company reflects the philosophy established by the founders, based on Psalm 68:11,
"The Lord gave the word and great was the company of those who published it."

Book design copyright © 2010 by Tate Publishing, LLC. All rights reserved.
Cover design by Amber Gulilat
Interior design by Stephanie Woloszyn

Published in the United States of America

ISBN: 978-1-61663-372-1
Religion / Christian Life / Spiritual Growth
10.06.24

about the Author

Thomas Herrington holds a B.A. in history, a Master of Arts in the Teaching of Foreign Language and a certificate of study from Peking University. He is an ELL teacher with the Oxford School District and has had the opportunity to go on volunteer trips to Cambodia and China. He lives with his beautiful wife and son in Oxford where he continues to live out this wonderful journey called life.

table of Contents

today I give up
My Rights

Today I will cease to look for justice, but never cease to give it.

Today I will cease to look for righteousness in others, but never cease to pursue it.

Today I will cease to defend myself, but never cease to allow hurt, injury, and insult to become opportunities in which I can display the love, affection, and mercy of my Lord, Jesus Christ.

Today I will cease to be impatient with others and when more is asked of me, I will give without holding back.

Today I will cease to put my hand to the plow and look back, but rather I will run hard the race set before me and run as if to get the prize.

Today I will cease seeking what I want for myself, but rather I will look within to see what more I can give to help, support, and carry others in their struggles.

Today I will cease to treat God as a habit, a chore, or a crutch, but rather I will seek him as a lover, as the Creator and Lord he is and never think twice before following.

Today I will cease allowing the devil to bring up my past mistakes, but rather look to Christ and know that within I am made anew and that all is well with my soul.

Today I will cease trying to do things the way I want to do them, but rather seek wisdom and direction before taking a step in what I think is the right direction.

Today I will cease trying to do the things that I want to do, but rather search out what is wanted for me and thus acknowledge what God wants for me is better than what I want for myself.

Today I will cease trying to win the world, but rather I will go, knowing that all that is required has been done and just seek to serve, love, and share what God has done for me.

Today I will cease saying what I think is best or trying to speak persuasive arguments, but rather I will yearn to listen to the Holy Spirit and wait on his words that will come from him, through me, to the listener. In doing so, I will acknowledge that the simplest phrase uttered by listening to the Holy Spirit is more powerful than the most persuasive oration of man.

Today I will cease seeing people and this world the way I perceive them. I will not see faces, but hearts; I will not see bodies, but rather eternal souls that my Savior, Jesus Christ, has paid for in full. I will not see myself, but rather see an instrument, continually being sharpened, formed, and used for those whom I meet.

Today I will cease hearing people the way I perceive them, but rather I will hear hopes and dreams rather than laughter, I will hear sorrows and cries for help rather than crying, and I will hear the desire within each person to know true hope, true love, true joy—truth, rather than hearing nonchalant questions.

the spiritual wonders
of Kayaking

I love the water. If I had my druthers, I would live aboard a sailboat or houseboat and refer to myself as "captain." In fact, I would have a delightful time figuring out what name I would emblazon upon my craft and also have a dinghy with an equally appropriate name. I just learned to sail, so I doubt that I will be circumnavigating the globe any time soon, but I do dream of performing that great task.

One summer, these desires found themselves nearer reality than before—I found myself working at a beachside resort in Pass Christian, Mississippi. The water was all around, beckoning me to conquer. I am sure the way I felt was similar to the way early explorers felt as they viewed the Atlantic Ocean, wondering what was on the other side. Not that I did not know what was on the other side—Bay St. Louis was on the other side—but it was still a monumental task for a beginner as myself. West of the resort, in Bay St. Louis, one could easily see Our Lady of the Bay, a beautiful Catholic church breaching the skyline with its bell tower. Separating Our Lady of the Bay and where I stood was a bay that was about two miles wide. Yes, I would conquer this bay before I left for the summer, so my imagination began plotting and scheming how I would leave this resort as a victorious explorer.

After thinking about the task, I drove off to Wendy's to dine from the .99 cent value menu, and I reset the odometer on my truck to measure the approximate distance across the bay. On the other side, munching on a junior bacon cheeseburger, I started a mental checklist of what I would need:

Boat

Paddle

Life jacket—a very good life jacket

Flares? Hmm, maybe.

Radio for the coast guard? I read this story once...

And a set of cool sailing flags so I could spell something. No, too much.

Luckily, on the way back from Wendy's on Highway 90 there is a K-Mart. It had been years since I had gone to a K-Mart, but this one was calling my name. As I entered, I realized what I had been missing—all K-Marts have this particular smell. I am not sure what it is, but I surmise that K-Mart bottles the stuff because all of them smell the same. While wondering about the particular smell and why the old one in Columbia smelled the same way, I made my way back to the sporting goods section and there, snuggled in between sleeping bags and camp cookware, I found my boat: an inflatable kayak made by Coleman. Not only was it in "easy-to-see-if-lost-at-sea-yellow," but it was a two-seater. Yes, that would do. After checking out, I brought my new prized possession to my truck and drove off to the resort.

Upon reaching the resort, I tried out my idea on a few of the locals. A friend of mine, Robert (he is from St. Tammany parish, so I often called him St. Tammany) did not know what to think of the idea. I told him I got the two-seater kayak because if I am going to die doing something stupid, I might as well have company. Misery loves company, so why doesn't a bad idea love company? It made sense to me.

"I don't know, the pictures just show really calm water, and the water out there isn't very calm." Robert was speaking in a voice that I never liked that much: the voice of reason. Yes, it was hurricane season, and yes, we have had thunderstorms every afternoon, but those were minor details. Water spouts are slower than tornados anyway, I reasoned. Despite worries from a rational mind, my dream persevered.

Later that week, I went to a store in Gulfport called Academy Sports. Now that place is for the serious sportsman. There were real kayaks—not the kind that need an air compressor—but bona fide kayaks. They also had really good life jackets, not those sissy kind that are hunter's orange and as comfortable as a t-shirt made with sandpaper, but neat vests with all of the bells and whistles. They had some that inflated—just one rip on a cord—similar to the kind that you find on a 747. (I have always wanted to steal one of those because the many times I have flown, we never used them.) They also had several vests made for paddling. I figured that is what I needed even though it didn't have a cool strobe light like some of the ones in the store. Walking out of the store, my mind should have registered something was a little out of whack when my life jacket cost almost as much as the boat I would be in, but that, of course, was a small detail.

I must admit all of this isn't as spontaneous as I would want to let you believe. I did already own a kayak paddle. One year prior, the Wal-Mart in Hattiesburg had a kayak paddle on sale for ten dollars, so I purchased it. Destiny was calling me to the water.

Months later, I was living on the coast and I had a kayak paddle, pfd, and an inflatable kayak. After opening the box, I discovered that the kayak came with two paddles. I had three kayak paddles—two for the paddlers and a spare. The dream was on the verge of reality.

June in Mississippi is not the best of all months. It rains everyday, which makes one wonder why people always talk of June brides—it would just rain on every wedding if they had them. Every afternoon, without fail, it would rain and thwart our efforts to take a practice run into the bay. Kyle the musician (he is a musician and one day will be famous) liked the idea, and I now had an accomplice. Since it rained every afternoon, we decided the wisest thing was to take the kayak out at night. Well, perhaps that was not the wisest thing, but it was convenient. The wind was atrocious—in fact, I got scared a few times. Waves would come over the bow of the boat, and it felt that we were working our arms off and not going anywhere. It took more effort than I had imagined, but finally we returned to shore. It took so much effort, that it made me wonder how anything ever washes up to shore, because we were definitely being pulled away from shore.

After the first trial run, I was a little skeptical of our ability to make it across the bay within a twenty-four hour period (before, I had estimated it would take thirty minutes), but Kyle the musician remained optimistic. His optimism helped keep the dream alive, so I looked forward to another day when the waves would be conquered.

A week later, the weather seemed to be permitting (meaning that lightning strikes were an hour apart), and I came to the staff house seeking Kyle the musician. Since he was nowhere to be found, St. Tammany (who was playing Halo) seemed like a great person to be lost at sea with. He seemed keen to the idea, so I ran down the hall, grabbed my life jacket, and met him in the parking lot where we aired up the boat. In conversation, as we made our way to the water, I found out that he had never canoed before, much less kayaked. Although he had not done these things, he had a great sense of humor and would make the journey an adventure. So we journeyed on.

After double checking the valves to make sure we would not deflate mid-voyage, we set sail and immediately headed in towards the north side of the bay. We headed that way because the wind picked up and pushed us that way. Despite the fact that the direction we were heading was not of our own volition, it seemed like we were kayaking and continued on.

When we tried to change our direction or tried to head back to where we came from, we went all over the place. Kayaking in the sea with a harsh wind did things to our kayak that made us look like drunken sailors. We went in circles most of the time, and when we were going straight, we would laugh until we started circling again. I felt more like a turkey buzzard than the professional kayaker I imagined I was. To add insult to injury, Robert's paddle lost both of its blades. It is hard to kayak in the ocean when all you have is a pole.

Shaken, we eventually made it back to the shore a little more concerned on how much the Coast Guard would get involved in our endeavor. As we reached the shore, Robert got out and retrieved his shoes that he had left on the shore. While waiting, I paddled out a little ways. In that short distance I discovered something—it was much easier to paddle by myself. With only one person in the kayak, the kayak stayed farther out of the water, reduced friction, and was a lot easier to move around. In fact, the difference was so great, there was really no comparison. An idea lurked in the back of my head that I must go solo.

As time went on, life got busy and soon I procrastinated until the last minute—my kayaking career is a close parallel of my academic career. I found myself two days before I was supposed to leave to go to school and still, as of yet, had not crossed the bay. I was determined to cross the bay—by myself this time—so I got my gear together and swung by the snack shack at the resort.   Working the snack shack were Dr. Amber and Nathan Luter. Nathan Luter (we all called him Luter) is perhaps one of the most genuine people I know. He doesn't tell a lie, even when most people would say you should. He was a loyal friend, so I gave him the responsibility to call the police, Coast Guard, or whomever if I did not return within a four-hour period. I told him approximately where I would be and, if he got a chance, to glance to see if there was an easy-to-see-if-lost-at-sea-yellow kayak in the bay.

At that, I got in my truck and drove across the bay and parked near the Our Lady of the Bay church. I was so determined to make the trip that I failed to plan any aspect of it other than to have a boat, life jacket, and paddle. I didn't bring water, sunscreen, or any other item that common sense would dictate as a need. I was still wearing my staff shirt, a pair of long pants (they were Ex Officio—my favorite brand of clothing—this way if I got lost at sea, at least I would have a lot of cool pockets on my pants) and sandals. I had a cell phone and a rechargeable air compressor. I left my keys in my truck (you can still do that in some places in Mississippi) and marched off to the beckoning sea.

The beach was crowded—more crowded than any other time that summer. It was Fourth of July weekend, and people were enjoying the Friday (July 2nd) with family and friends. Since quite a few were enjoying beers and other stuff, I whispered a quiet prayer that a drunken boater wouldn't run over me, and I commenced airing up my raft. I don't know how Amelia Earhart or Christopher Columbus felt as they boarded their craft, but I sure hope they had more fanfare than I had. The only attention that I gathered was that of a preschooler who liked my inflatable kayak and a Yorkshire pup that felt threatened by my boat and was growling menacingly towards my kayak. Where were leash laws when you needed them? My destiny was about to be thwarted by a yippy mammal that weighed less than my paddle.

I climbed in my boat and set a nearby goal: the end of the fishing pier. The pier was pretty long, so I paddled to the end of it, enjoying the feel of paddling off into the ocean. As I reached the end of the pier, I decided it was time to rest—that is the good part about a boat—you can stop whenever you feel like it and enjoy the to and fro of the waves. I sat watching the fishermen on the pier, children with kites, a mother using a cast net—she caught a crab in one of her throws—and a father trying to fix his fancy Sea Doo that evidently wasn't working properly. As I sat their watching, I glanced up to see the sun shining and big, fluffy white clouds bounding past.

The only problem was that the only cloud I saw took up most of the horizon and was actually a black thunderhead. When you look up and see something as foreboding as that, the distance from where you are to the shore doesn't make much difference—you feel a little nervous.

A little disappointed, but more rational than usual, I paddled back to the shore—but stopped shy of the shoreline. I sat their bobbing in the water wondering what to do. I knew that the distance between the railroad bridge and the passenger car bridge was about half a mile, so I could feasibly go from bridge to bridge four times, go the distance required, and still be within reach of the safety that the shore offered. But what would that accomplish? I would stay five to ten yards from the shore and go back and forth, and not get as far as a child could chasing an overthrown Frisbee.

Well, I did not know what to do, so I started paddling for the passenger vehicle bridge. After a while, I reached the bridge and went under it to the northern side. This, of course, was not where I told Luter to look for me, but I would worry about that later. While I was on the northern side of the bridge, I immediately noticed two things that were different—the bridge helped break up the waves, so they were not as formidable, and the wind was not as vicious. With these two factors, it did not take too much consideration: I would continue on the northern side of the bridge. At this point of the trip, I had left my original route, left my partner, and yet, still had not left the shore. I looked up to see clouds dissipating (if it does not rain real quickly, the Mississippi heat will often push off rain clouds) and I had my chance to leave the shore.

So, there I went, paddling off into the water, adrenaline pumping, arms churning, straight ahead across the bay. As I kept going across the bay, it was rather hard to keep a straight line; as waves would come, my boat would change direction, go sideways, or turn in a circle. Plus, if I stopped, it seemed to take more energy to get back up to speed than I gained in resting for a minute or two. As I continued my trek across the bay, I constantly wanted to turn back and look to see how far I had progressed. And each time I would start to turn my head, I would think, *Do you really want to know?* The thought of knowing exactly how far I was from safety was not as comforting as the knowledge of how far I had traversed. For this reason, I kept my head straight ahead, not glancing in the opposite direction.

As I continued kayaking, I came across four motorboats that were anchored and one kayak crossed my path. The ones in the motorboats looked at me as if I were out of my mind. They sat in their comfortable chairs in boats that had more horsepower than many tow-trucks, with a beer in one hand and a fishing pole in the other, gawking at me as I went by. I guess they did not know what to think of me. As for the kayak that crossed my path, they (there were two people in this kayak; it also was a real kayak) looked at me, smiled and nodded, and continued paddling. They understood. Yes, we were crazy, but we were enjoying our craziness. I understood them—they did not waste their breath speaking—too much energy was required by the task at hand. They continued, headlong into the wind as I crossed perpendicular to their path, both boats' occupants cheered on by the sight of a kindred spirit seeking to conquer the waves.

Once I passed the draw bridge, I came across another obstacle: jet skis. What is the deal with those people? You would think after the eight-millionth time they drove in a circle, they would get tired of it. No, not at all. They kept going back and forth, back and forth, as a child would stay on a "sit-and-spin" until he fell off from dizziness. I also assumed that they would slow down for the guy in the inflatable kayak, but that was not the case. They would pass, staring at me, grinning, as they sped by. They viewed me like some redneck driving a four-by-four pick-up views a possum crossing the highway. That far out from shore, I was having to battle three-foot waves. With a jet ski blitzing by, the waves would reach four feet—a wave large enough that I could not see where I was going because I would be staring at the inside of my kayak. That was a little unnerving, but if I kept paddling, the water would not come in the boat.

As the jet skis kept speeding by, I would occasionally envy them, but then I would try to make up some excuse. "This is good exercise. Those jerks don't care about the environment. Don't they have something better to do? I am accomplishing something. They are not. Jerks. If they had not been jerks, I would have asked them to fetch me a bottle of water. I only spent one hundred dollars on my boat. They should have bought a cheap boat and given the money to the poor. If I had a harpoon…" I had to stop myself. I would talk for days about them—one reason being that I did not have anyone else to talk to. I needed to stop because they thought I was crazy to begin with—and for me to be glaring at them, muttering to myself, hollering out something about World Vision or the Salvation Army or Green Peace did not make matters better.

Despite the distractions of jet skis, fishermen, crab traps (I was afraid of what one of those would do to the bottom of my boat, so I often had to steer clear of them), and the wind, I soon made it to the far side of the shore. In less than an hour and a half, I accomplished something that took the majority of the summer to mull over in my mind, preoccupy my thoughts, and incite spats of daydreaming. An hour and a half. Afterwards, I wore my life jacket all the way inside the building, just to spur people to ask what great deed I had accomplished. I even looked in the mirror at some muscle that was bulging out on my shoulders—evidently there is a particular muscle that one uses to paddle that you do not normally use. At least that is what I told myself when my shoulders would cramp up. So within less than two hours, I had achieved my summer dream and, if you must know, it was sort of anticlimactic, similar to my undergraduate commencement ceremonies.

What I learned from the small trip across the bay:

In everything that we do, there is a lesson waiting to be learned. Whether we learn from making a poor decision or by making the right decision, there is still an apt lesson to be learned. In this excursion across the bay, I discovered several truths that can be applied to our walk with our Creator.

First, sometimes we need to get rid of things that will weigh us down. Although I wanted company as I crossed the bay, the additional weight made the kayak nearly impossible to navigate. The same goes for our lives—we fill our ship full of things to "aid" us in our journey. We bring the past, our failures, our pride, and so much more "stuff" that weighs us down and does not help in the efficiency and tranquility of our journey. Jesus knows that while we try to traverse our journeys in this life, we would grow weary from bearing the weight of our desires. He called upon us asking for us to come to him and receive his yoke: "My burden is easy, my burden is light."[1]

Upon commissioning the disciples, Jesus told them to depart and bring nothing for their journey—except a mere staff. "No bread, no bag, no money in their belt"[2]—what was he thinking? Perhaps he knew what was on the other side. Perhaps he knew his Father well enough to trust God to provide. Perhaps his wisdom was not of this world—not of keeping everything until we are wearied beyond what we can bear—but rather finding wisdom that sees yielding in submission to a perfect Father as the most rational and freeing thought.

The second lesson that I learned is that sometimes we must go alone. I am an introvert to a degree, but I do not like doing things by myself. I am always surrounded by others—and with these others, I have developed dependencies through various friendships. When I find myself away from all others, I find out who I really am—not who I am within a certain paradigm, party, or clique—but who I am with everything else stripped away. In the "alone" moments of our lives, God teaches us a lot about ourselves and these lessons may be missed if we are surrounded by others.

If Robert and I had taken off across the bay together and we failed in that attempt—I could have walked away satisfied, knowing that it was not me, but the other party that failed. When we are alone, stripped from our worldly dependencies, we have to face our circumstances with an uncomfortable vulnerability. Jesus marched off alone multiple times—each time he left to speak with his Father. His relationship, just like ours, was between him and his Father. The disciples did not make Jesus's relationship with his father more important, tangible, or easy. The disciples probably made Jesus's relationship with the father more difficult if anything. It was in those "alone" moments where Jesus recharged his batteries and was able to face the world again.

On the journey, we will find our relationship with God strengthened and our soul challenged yet refreshed when we find these alone moments with God. God understands human nature and knows how we often try to form dependencies with those around us; even though we know that they will inevitably fail us. The relationship that God seeks to have with us is only between God and the individual—God seeks for us to be with Him and to be still. It is in those still moments that we come to know that He is God.[3]

The next lesson came out of my lack of planning, but it is an important lesson nonetheless. When I had made it half way out into the bay, I started to get really thirsty. Since my crossing the bay involved more daydreaming than planning, I neglected to bring drinking water for my voyage. The ironic part was that I just wanted one sip of water, and I was surrounded by water that I could not drink. Many times, we seek after things that resemble what we need, but in the end, the things we see in abundance are not good for us and do not help us complete the journey. The water around me was just like any other water with just one exception—it had salt in it. How many times do we as an individual, and as an integral part of the body of Christ, partake in something that is in abundance, that resembles what we need, but in the end is not good for us?

What is needed versus what is readily available is seen in the story of Mary and Martha. What was really evident to Martha is that there were guests and food needed to be prepared. What was waiting to be seen is what Mary chose—that which was important and would not be taken away from her. God knows what we need. He promises that he will provide.

How do we find what God seeks to give us? It is simple: "Seek first his kingdom and his righteousness, and all these things will be added to you."[4] The idea is not "settle for what is closest and most convenient and perhaps you can add more stuff later." Just like me on the ocean waves, I was surrounded by what appeared to suffice, but the intended blessing and glory awaited me at the end of the journey.

The fact that waves get big seems like a no-brainer, but I discovered the true size of the waves when I was riding them in a small boat rather than when I glanced upon them from the shore. The waves near the shore paled in comparison to those that awaited me when I got out in the middle of the bay. Away from the safety provided by the shore, I found myself buffeted by waves that were larger than I could have imagined. Not only were there waves around me, but there were also waves created by other people around me. The people who were cruising by in their enormous boats or fast jet skis rocked my boat until the journey was harder than it should have been. In our lives, we should expect the waves to shake us—for storms will come and will often find us when we are far from safety—but we must not change our course. These storms may come in the shape of a bad situation at work, problems with the kids, or something tragic, but we should hold our course regardless of what is tossed upon us. Paul said that we should run the race—to go full speed ahead, surrounded by this crowd of witnesses.[5] Paul had so many bad things happen to him, he had to alphabetize the list in a Rolodex just to keep up with it all. And yet he didn't waver. It is hard; it gets harder at times, but the waves are just a nuisance in the journey, not the journey itself. Do not waver and run the race.

While on the journey, look around and see those who share your same vision and hope. If you haven't found out already, those who are on your side will not create waves to steer you off course, but rather give you encouragement. While kayaking, people who were like me in their mission did not create waves. Other kayakers went by without creating havoc, without the smell and noise of a V8, and without hindering me in my journey.

Peter faced the same thing when he walked out on the sea. The waves looked a lot less intimidating from the security of a fisherman's vessel, but through his experience he also learned how to stay the course and enjoy the comforts of fellow travelers. As he stepped out of the boat, he knew that the waves were big, but he also knew what was in front of him, a loving Savior, and what was behind him, those fellow travelers that watched and encouraged him as he took his first step.

When I would see other kayakers paddling onward, I was reassured that what I was attempting was possible. The same goes for us with our spiritual walk. Look around and find that silent encouragement from others that whispers, "I'm struggling too, but we will make it." Just as their journey speaks to you, your endurance speaks volumes to the weary souls around you as well.

The fifth lesson deals with communication: even if you think that the reception will be bad, make contact. When I was out in the water, I was hesitant to contact Luter on my cell phone because I was afraid I would attempt to call, the reception would be bad, or Luter would misunderstand me and then do something rash like call the police. Then I would have caused more problems than if I would not have called in the first place. This lesson can be applied to two different parts of life. The first is our relationship with God and the second deals with our relationships with others.

Often when I find myself off course in my spiritual life, I swallow the lie that I should not ask God for help because he will be ashamed, embarrassed, or angry. When I find myself, once again drenched in my sinful nature, I start thinking, "Oh, no, I did it now. I'm far from God. Steered too far away. If I try to talk to him, he may not even hear me, and even if he did, I wouldn't want to face him like this. No, not right now. Later, when I am better. When I am closer to shore, then I will contact him." And thus I don't contact the one who is looking out for me. I have a tendency to misconstrue who God is by fearing that God is this extremely disappointed entity that is waiting for me to screw up just so he can administer swift and crushing retaliation. The image of who God is presented in Hebrews is very different from the one I am often afraid to face. "Approach the throne of grace with confidence."[6] Confidence? I have messed up everything; I can not fix it; and now I go to someone perfect and ask for help? No way. But Christ is our high priest who can sympathize with our weaknesses. He is a redeemer that wants us to come to him with confidence, so we may "receive mercy and find grace to help us in our time of need."[7] The same goes with relationships—a broken father/son relationship often can be fixed with a simple phone call, but the worries come, "If I try to talk to him, he may not even hear me and even if he did…" Regardless of how far we have gone, we need to contact him. He hears us.[8]

The last lesson is the journey itself. When I grew up, I heard fathers telling sons about their lives growing up: "I walked six miles to school, in the snow, uphill, both ways." I could relate when I was kayaking across the bay—there was no gradual incline or decline that I could get used to or plan on, but a constant pulling and pushing in every direction. Uphill both ways. Nobody said it would be easy, Jesus included. Although life will be difficult, we have a Savior who is "faithful and just to complete the work that he began in us."[9] Not only is Christ with us in the journey, not only does he help us with our journey, but he is our journey. "I am the way, the truth and the life. No man comes to the father except by me."[10]

So when the storms come and the waves knock you back and forth, keep straight and run the race set before you. Your Savior is with you, helping you and loving you dearly.

God bless and happy kayaking.

fruit drinks and
Christians

The other day I stopped in at a truck stop because my truck and I were thirsty. Of course my truck drank about forty dollars worth, whereas I only drank three bucks worth.

After many years of road trips, I developed a system of staying awake and how to enjoy my beverages on the road. Out of habit, I quickly went by the Cokes and picked up a one-liter of Sprite. Then in an attempt to be healthy, I grabbed a one-liter of bottled water. As I was leaving, I saw some fruit juices, so I grabbed a "fruit punch" beverage. The front of the label proclaimed "made with real fruit juice," so I bought it.

Climbing back into my truck, I looked at my three choices and carefully selected what I would drink first. I don't really like cold water, so I would let it sit for a while. As for the Sprite, it is okay if it isn't really cold (if it was a Coke, I would have drunk it first). I grabbed the fruit punch and took a swig. I immediately knew I had been swindled. It tasted more like liquid candy than it did like fruit juice. I turned the bottle around, so I could read the rest of the label—"3 % Fruit Juice." I felt deceived. On the front, it had "made with real fruit juice" in a nifty font upon a wavy, pretty colored background. Then on the back, just above NUTRITIONAL INFORMATION was the percentage of fruit juice. As I drove up

I-55, I pondered the irony of my "made with real fruit juice" drink. That is sort of like a contractor saying that he is going to build a person a brick house, but only puts bricks on the front steps. What is that about?

What I learned from my fruit juice

At times I am a lot like that fruit drink. I am a Christian, but are there times when people see me and I am running more like 3% than 100%? I am sure that happens more times than I would like to admit. The problem with Christians is that we don't have the disclaimer printed on our backs that we are having a bad day, or week, or year for that matter. I am a Christian, and that label goes wherever I go. When people see me, they see Thomas, a Christian.

Sermons can be just like my fruit juice as well. Many times sermons contain more cute stories or jokes and sayings than God's word. If pastors taught God's word without all of the filler, sermons would be more like 100% Bible than just 3%.

If we and our pastors changed, I am sure that the difference would not go without notice.

Jesus taught that we must deny ourselves, take up our cross daily and follow Him. If we deny ourselves, we put ourselves in a position where we will be filled with God. Often I am only "3%" Christian because I failed to deny myself—when God tried to fill me with his wisdom, joy, and truth, I had little room due to my selfishness, earthly desires, and slothfulness.

If you find yourself more like the 3% Christian, the first place to look is your walk. If I claim to be a Christian and I slack a little bit and don't read my Bible all week, my relationship will suffer. To compensate for being a slacker, I am sure to go to church on Sunday morning and Wednesday night and say an extra long prayer before going to bed since I couldn't squeeze God in during the morning. If that was my week, how about we see what kind of walk with Christ that is? If God counts time with him in prayer like my cell phone company counts minutes of usage, I probably could get by in saying I pray three minutes each meal—three meals a day (who am I kidding? I never wake up in time to eat breakfast) at seven days a week—twenty-one times three is sixty-three minutes or one hour and three minutes. My five minute nightly prayers and the Sunday morning and Wednesday night bring my grand total to three hours and thirty-eight minutes. Hmm. Three hours and thirty-eight minutes out of 168 hours in the week. That means I am giving God approximately 2% of my time. Now if I can somehow put that into perspective and realize that I am giving a gracious, loving, all-powerful God that spared nothing, including his son, to show me love, grace, and mercy, 2% of my time—should I be surprised when people encounter me and find me weak, just as I did that fruit juice?

If we find ourselves running on about 2%, perhaps we need to find truth in the statement "if salt loses its saltiness then it is only to be thrown out and trampled." Salt that isn't salty, fruit drinks that aren't fruity, and Christians who aren't "Christian" are all equally useless.

the fried
Potato Girl

I must tell you where I was when I saw her. I was eating at a fine eating establishment called "Lambert's" in Foley, Alabama, also known as the "Home of Throwed Rolls." A restaurant that is as excellent as Lambert's does not need to worry itself with cumbersome things like grammar because the proof is in the pudding, or rolls and home-style cooking. Why are they known as the "home of throwed rolls"? Well, it is probably what you are thinking. Yes, they throw rolls. That expression, "pass the roll" is taken very literally at Lambert's, and that has become part of their popularity. When a patron wants a hot, steamy roll, all he must do is raise his hand and a server will rear back and throw a roll the size of a softball to him. This really enhances the eating atmosphere. I believe that when you have to go for a pass to catch part of your meal, it seems more gratifying when you take a bite. Similar to a hunter bringing game to the table, I can proudly bring a roll to the table because I caught it.

Another feature to the restaurant is that they have "pass-arounds." These are side items that come with your meal, and servers walk around with big, cast-iron pots of black-eyed peas, macaroni, or fried potatoes and, upon your request, will heap them upon your plate. These uniform-clad servers never stop walking round and round the restaurant, ceaselessly piling more and more food on your plate. So about the fried potato girl…

The young lady would enter each section of the restaurant and offer fried potatoes to the customers as she would pass their tables, calling to them with three words everyone loves to hear: "more fried potatoes?" As delicately as a young lady clad in overalls and a flannel shirt and wielding a cast-iron pot can, she would smile, nod, and serve massive amounts of fried potatoes to anyone who answered her call. This particular day, I am sure the black-eyed peas girl and the macaroni girl were jealous because the fried potatoes were definitely the favorite in our section of the restaurant.

A middle-aged man who was sitting across the restaurant from me would get helpings every time she passed. He ate more potatoes than I thought were humanly possible. As soon as the announcement, "Fried potatoes!" was made, the man would get a glisten in his eye to match the grease glistening on his chin, and watch the corner of the far aisle for the fried potato girl to appear. He waited for her to round the corner like a small child peering into the living room on Christmas Eve waiting on St. Nick. As she would round the corner, his eyes would grow larger and he would watch as she made her way down the aisle. His jaw would drop a little and his face would quiver as he fought the urge to blink, as if he were afraid that if he blinked, the potatoes would disappear.

"Fried potatoes! Fried potatoes. Fried potatoes?" He nodded in silence, as if the ambience was now very holy and to speak would somehow violate this magical moment. Nodding emphatically as she heaped fried potatoes upon his plate, his expression thanked her better than eloquent words could ever express. As she left, he nodded once more and sat in silence for a few seconds eyeing the potatoes. After this moment of silence, he smiled and then started wolfing down the potatoes without hesitation, because he knew that there were more helpings to come.

Watching him with those potatoes told the truth about the situation: it really wasn't about the girl after all. It did not matter what she looked like or who her daddy was or how much money she made—it was about what she did and what she had to offer. What she did so entranced this man that he would stare into space, waiting oh-so-patiently, waiting for a glimpse of that unwieldy, cast-iron pot of potatoes. It was not the promise of more, but the actual provision. It was not the amount given, but the assurance that the supply was endless.

This girl stayed constant, walking up and down the aisle, offering to all of those present what she possessed—fried potatoes. To those that had plenty, she still offered. And to those that refused her each time she passed, she still gave them a chance to accept her offer the next time she came by. It was all she had, but she gave it liberally.

What happened in this restaurant is what should happen within the church. We should not sneak around like door-to-door vacuum cleaner salesmen or be flamboyant orators about the glory to come, but we should just show up with what God gives and give it without expectation, hesitation, or prejudice.

We, as Christians, have nothing to sell or promote—it is free. It is not about who we are, although many of us wish it were. It is not in the presentation—just simple, constant giving. An unending supply of God's love to those around us is what is needed. That's all. And that is what will leave them waiting for someone who is in love with Christ to round the corner—because they know what is in store.

possum
Diaries

One day I was driving back from Wal-Mart with one of my Korean roommates, Kunman, when we narrowly missed a possum. It bolted from the tree line onto our street, and I swerved and hit the brakes right before what I thought was imminent impact. There was no resounding thud, but my car and possum came so close that I thought I should stop and see if it was anywhere around. I was afraid that the animal would be cowering under the car and would be hit when I drove off. All of what happened I didn't think to explain to my roommate. Possums were pretty common in Mississippi and part of my upbringing; however, my roommate had never seen a possum before—I could tell by the way he reacted. When I stopped, he pulled his feet up from the floorboard and hugged his knees as if the possum would somehow bite his feet off after clawing its way through the floorboard (his pose was very similar to the way I sat after watching Stephen King's movie, *Kujo*).

Before that moment, I never thought how strange a possum must look to a person who had never seen one before. Kunman's reaction declared that such creatures do not exist on the busy boulevards of Daejeon, South Korea. His reaction also showed that he thought it was an animal that was not normal and should be feared. My guess is that he thought it was a very, very large rat. Well, if

I thought a rat was that big, I would be scared, too, so I didn't open the door of the car and slowly started our way back home. As I drove, I started thinking about how strange it must be to see a possum and think, "oh, that's normal." I came to this consensus after trying to tell Kunman that, in fact, it wasn't a rat, but rather a distant relative of the kangaroo.

"It is a marsupial, not a rodent or whatever. Sort of like a kangaroo," I explained.

"Kangaroo. Kangaroo?" his voice raised in pitch that communicated that I had failed in trying to ease his fears.

"Well, kind of. You know, it sticks its babies in a pouch after they are born… you can fit about twenty of 'em in a tablespoon because they are so small when they are born."

"A kangaroo?" he asked. He nervously glanced back behind our car and then up around the tree line as if they could now leap from the tops of the trees that lined the street. I thought that the kangaroo comparison was confusing for him, so I thought I would clear things up by saying it didn't jump, but it does have a prehensile tail.

"Present mile?" he asked.

"No, prehensile."

"How do you spell it?" he inquired.

"I don't know how to spell it. You know, like a monkey. It can use its tail like we use our hands—it can grab things like a tree branch and whatnot."

"A monkey?" he asked. He waved his hand around as if it was a swinging tail with fingers attached. He looked out the window again, peered intensely into the darkened silhouettes of pines and sweet gum trees, checked the lock on the door, and looked forward.

"No, no, not a monkey. Not like that. Umm, maybe like a nice rat, but it has a set of teeth like a dog. Something strange though, a possum doesn't have enamel on its teeth. If it were to bite down hard on your leg, it really hurts itself too." At that, he looked at me, his body cringing, and gave me a questioning look as if we were soon to be consumed by the creature at large in our neighborhood.

"Not a dog, maybe more like a cat. One time, when I was little,

I scared one and it hissed at me—woo—I jumped and ran back in the house as fast as I could. They look scary, but really they aren't *that* bad."

I think he understood that description well enough because he started looking out the window nervously and upon our arrival to our house, he looked out the door and then leapt from the car as if the creature had somehow clung to the vehicle to devour us upon our arrival home. It's a good thing we didn't see a bobcat or an armadillo (those things can give you leprosy—imagine having to explain that).

Through this multicultural, marsupial experience, I discovered that what is common for one person is very strange and confusing for another. Possums in Mississippi are pretty common. They roam about at night munching on whatever they can find. Is that normal? To me it was quite ordinary to see one of these creatures crossing the road; to my roommate, however, he thought it was quite out of the ordinary and probably had nightmares about these gigantic rats that jump like kangaroos and swing like monkeys from tree to tree.

The way I treated the possum crossing the road is the same way the church treats many customs that they do—as ordinary. But outsiders—people looking from the outside into the church—must think that the things we do are a little strange. We need to *explain* to them what we do. We have the Lord's supper. Why? We give a tithe. Why? We baptize or christen people. Why? What is a soul? When the church speaks of the "soul," is that the same as when someone talks about their "soul mate" or when I listen to a song by Soul Asylum or any other band with "soul" in their name?

I think these questions are of merit—both for them to ask of us and also for us to ask ourselves. Until I understand the how, why, and what of our traditions and beliefs, I will be inept and inefficient in communicating what I know and believe to others. If a Korean is to explain why his country has a certain custom, he will need to start from scratch when he discusses it with me. The same goes for me when I try to explain an indigenous animal or a religious festival or custom. Many internationals know equally as much about a possum as they do about Jesus. And until that lack of knowledge is replaced with answers that they understand, they will react towards what I believe with trepidation and disbelief.

sciurus
Caroliniensis

My mother's father, whom I affectionately called "Papa," waged a war his entire life. I am not sure when it started, but I am sure it started way before he tried to join the ranks of the Marines in the '40s. Perhaps it began when he was a child growing up in southern Georgia; a conflict inherited from his father. I am not sure when it started, but I know the war only ended when they laid my Papa in his grave while his enemies watched from a safe distance near a stalwart long oak tree.

I am not sure *why* it started as well. Perhaps it was because he had an innate hatred for the poor creatures, or perhaps he liked having a formidable enemy that would give him a challenge and, perhaps, a purpose. Whatever the motivation was, it had to be a strong one because I never knew a time when the battle wasn't raging at 2102 Sterling Drive. Even in my first memories as a small child, I remember the war. I would arrive at my Nana and Papa's house, come in the front door, and notice signs of conflict: a gleaming Smith & Wesson pistol polished to a sheen that only a person as OCD as my Papa could create, a pair of binoculars sitting conspicuously on the kitchen window ledge, and several reference books about the enemy laid out on the breakfast room table. No one really brought the hostilities up, and if anything was done, it was my mother who, as mothers do, would place the gleaming sidearm in a desk drawer out of reach of my small, cumbersome hands and then act as if nothing ever happened.

Early on, the city incorporated my grandparents' home, so shooting a .32 caliber pistol within the confines of his backyard was no longer an option. I am sure the neighbors felt rather relieved, but my Papa took it as a personal insult and felt like his enemy had formed a military alliance. How was he supposed to defeat his enemy if his enemy had the protection of Uncle Sam? Since the enemy achieved sudden immunity from black powder projectiles, my Papa had to contemplate two other possible solutions: booby traps or an air gun. The booby traps would just catch his enemy for later release into another demilitarized zone, and he figured that would only let them regroup for another assault. The air gun would not guarantee certain death for his foe, but going for the greater of two evils, he decided that an air gun would at least allow him to be proactive in defending his base, which was made up of a 1960's-era, ranch-style house and three city lots filled with massive oak trees. Soon the shiny pistol was only seen when my Papa was cleaning it and a new Daisy .177 air-rifle found residence leaning up against the crank-open windows in the sun-room. The counter-insurgency was now down-sizing due to circumstances out of its control.

I knew my Papa had lost a lot of joy due to the transition. No more would that resounding explosion sound out to the neighborhood that another enemy was KIA, but rather neighbors would mistake the *flooomph* of an air gun for someone dropping the greater metropolitan area phonebook or for the shutting of a car door. I am sure his disappointment reflected how a despot must feel when the United Nations imposes economic sanctions against an unsympathetic ruler or perhaps that of a spoiled child who was told that he could not have another toy. This, in combination of his declining health, led to fewer and fewer attacks. Downtrodden, his attempts to charge the door like a World War I troop exploding over the top of a trench were rarely seen. He would just eye his enemy from the sunroom as he slowly ate his perfectly placed cereal (sugar first, bananas second, and cornflakes third). As eyesight dimmed and muscles atrophied, his shaking hands would reveal other battles being fought, and soon his enemy was making further advances into what used to be secure territory. Downtrodden, but not defeated, my Papa would glare back towards his enemy behind the safety of tinted Plexi-glass, plotting a Battle of the Bulge that would regain lost ground.

The last Christmas holidays we celebrated together were just like the ones that preceded it. That Christmas Eve, we placed gifts under the tree, stayed up talking about everything under the sun, and fell asleep around three to my Nana's watching Headline News at an excruciating volume level. The only difference seen or felt was that my Papa did not move about during the festivities. He would allow others to come to him and would sometimes get disoriented due to all of the confusion around him.

That next morning, we opened our presents and came to pause around breakfast in the sunroom. I never really liked Grape Nuts, and I wasn't really in the mood for corn flakes, so my only other option was to just watch everyone else eat as the crunch of Grape Nuts resounded like someone walking on pea gravel. I glanced across the room and did not see the air rifle and shrugged it off thinking it was put in a safe place out of the reach of my little cousins who were running around. I then looked outside to where the enemy was now frolicking about, not even thinking twice of their once formidable foe.

"One of them is on the bird feeder," I observed.

"I am certainly amazed at how they do that," my Nana mused. "We tried everything—even put those sheets of tin around the feeder and now just look. They jump down from the roof."

While everyone started gazing at the bird feeder, my Papa slowly put his spoon down, took a slow sip of orange juice and twisted around—not to look at the bird feeder, but to reach for an extension cord coming from outside the house. When he plugged it in, we all saw where the other end of the extension cord went. The poor squirrel never saw it coming. One hundred and ten volts rushed from the outlet of my Papa's sunroom along an extension cord that he had stripped bare to the top of the bird feeder to the little mammal's feet. I must admit I have never seen something so small leap so high, except for maybe a grasshopper. My parents didn't say anything. They probably couldn't think of anything to say after seeing my Papa attempt to electrocute the unsuspecting, furry mammal in his latest attempt to defend his home.

"Heh, heh, heh, cough, unh, heh, heh," my Papa, half wheezing, half laughing, smiled with contempt. "Must have been a new one. The ones that I've shocked before learn where the copper is and just dance around it. Smart little things."

At that, his frail hand picked up his spoon and he commenced eating his now soggy cereal. The rest of us just sat around staring at where the squirrel had been moments before, trying to grasp just how odd our family really was. I looked at my Papa, who was now enjoying his cereal more than before, and then glanced outside to the barren yard where squirrels looked down from the safety of their high perches. I looked back at my Papa and saw truth etched in the creases of his smile. Even if someone knows that they are going to lose the war, it still feels good to win a battle every now and then.

eating hot wings en route
to Grandmom's

On Father's Day of 2005, I woke up late and ended up leaving two and a half hours later than I intended for my return trip home. The result was that I was passing through Jackson, Mississippi, around 11:00 a.m., and I was really hungry. As I passed through Richland, I stopped at a large chain store to get gas and I bought some chicken wings. After getting fuel for me and my car, I drove on to my grandmom's house.

If you know anything about Sundays and grandmoms, you know that I was heading to my grandparents' to eat a Sunday lunch that is without comparison. And yet, my hunger and desire for fried foods drove me to buy some wings en route to the upcoming feast.

As I drove down the road toward my grandmother's house, I started thinking, *Well, I can just wait—throw the wings out or something.* But as the miles went by, I ended up peeling off the sticker that said "HONEY BBQ" and popped open the plastic container. Telling myself that I would have room for both these wings and lunch at Grandmom's house, I started munching down on one of the wings. Upon my first bite, I realized three things immediately:

These were not honey BBQ wings.

These were spicy wings.

These were very nasty spicy wings.

I have had many a hot wing from gas stations, church dinners, and homes, but the ones I bought on this trip were by far the worst I have ever tried. I wanted to throw them away and somehow ensure that the deli lady would pay for this mistake, but since I was already on the road—time was of the essence, and I didn't want to litter—I continued down the road with the nasty, spicy, gooey wings sitting on the console.

What was I thinking? I pondered. Those things were terrible and the food that waited on me at my grandmom's would be incredible.

But I am still hungry, I thought. As the trip went on, I would glance over and look at those nasty wings and think, *Well, they weren't that bad were they? I mean, I am really hungry. Just one more. Maybe it was just that one that was nasty. Maybe the rest are okay. I think I'll try it...* One by one, the chicken wings disappeared. One by one, napkins would get stuck to my fingers by the chicken wing goo. One by one, I would think that I just ate the nastiest hot wing in my life, but soon would justify eating another. By the end of the trip, I ended up eating the whole thing of chicken wings. The whole thing of wings that were *not* Honey BBQ. The whole thing of nasty hot wings.

While I tried dexterously to remove the napkin that was glued to my fingers from the hot wing goo, I pondered how stupid I must be to consume something I didn't like.

"What was I thinking?" I pondered out loud.

Well, just what was I thinking? Although I did not put it into words at that moment, I definitely was thinking about the immediate appeasement of an insatiable hunger versus waiting for something that was better and complete. Yes, I want it and I want it now. And this attitude is in no way a one time event. In fact, I think that statement can sum up most of our lives. And not only does it affect our personal lives, but also our spiritual lives as well. People often act on principles that they would not dare put into words: "I want to follow God, but the rewards come late in the game," "I need to check out what is in it for me," "I want a God who will redeem my reward points every three years or so, not some God that tells me it will be hard and that my reward is in heaven after I die. What is that about?" "'Store up your treasures in heaven'? What about my 401K, IRA, Roth IRA and money market accounts? Does God have a good interest rate?"

That is my mindset when it comes to following God, seeking his reward, and using self-discipline in seeking that reward. What is God's reward? That I am allowed to be in his presence and worship him. Keith Green summed it up in a song that all of his devotion would be given for an opportunity just to give glory to God. For someone, such as myself, who is self-seeking and wanting glory for himself, it would seem that I got the shaft when it came to rewards. Best Buy at least gives back 5% on their rewards program. Why can't God do that too? Or what about a punch card like they have at Subway, so I can get a blessing for every eight blessings I give—that would be great. But God is different. Very different—especially when compared to myself. My reward would be in front of me, ready to be expended the moment I was able to rest. My reward would be piecemeal, so it could appease my hunger for pride and honor as I went along the way. God's reward waits patiently at the end of the journey. Jesus told his followers that he was going to prepare a place for them. He said that when they get to heaven, the ones who looked after the least of these will hear "well done, good and faithful servant."

And just what sort of reward does God have to offer while we are wandering around trying to make sense of all of this? He says:

Blessed are the poor in spirit, for theirs is the kingdom of heaven. Blessed are those who mourn, for they shall be comforted. Blessed are the gentle, for they shall inherit the earth. Blessed are those who hunger and thirst for righteousness, for they shall be satisfied. Blessed are the merciful, for they shall receive mercy. Blessed are the pure in heart, for they shall see God. Blessed are the peacemakers, for they shall be called sons of God. Blessed are those who have been persecuted for the sake of righteousness, for theirs is the kingdom of heaven. Blessed are you when people insult you and persecute you, and falsely say all kinds of evil against you because of Me. Rejoice and be glad, for your reward in heaven is great; for in the same way they persecuted the prophets who were before you.[11]

Move your focus away from immediate desires and focus on the hand of God and where it is leading you. And you will find that "your reward in heaven" will be great.

driving without
Insurance

Finally, Mississippi joined a long list of states by passing a law requiring insurance. Before, if a driver did not have insurance, he just had to be careful that he did not ram into someone else while talking on his cell phone and driving erratically. With the new law in place, a driver will become the proud recipient of a one thousand dollar ticket if he can't prove that he has valid insurance.

After coming back from my teaching stint in China, I was now responsible for things like insurance, car notes, and other annoyances that come with becoming an adult. Evidently, I was enjoying these newfound freedoms, and I let my insurance slide a little. I was going to swap insurance companies, time got away from me, and the result was that my insurance ended before I started the new policy.

For those of you who haven't had a lapse in your insurance coverage, know that this was a bad idea. I didn't know until afterwards that insurance premiums jump if they see that a driver has a gap in his coverage. I think they should teach things like this in driver's education classes. I am sure the insurance companies were saying to themselves, "Now we have him where we want him, heh heh heh…" I had to get insurance and the companies knew I *had* to get it. As a result, the prices weren't too friendly.

Now driving illegally, I noticed that in just a few days, my driving changed. It was not drastic, but it changed nonetheless. I would still like to take curves a little too fast and be sure to rush through yellow lights, but not without a watchful eye. Every time I saw a cop, I went into this covert, super-sneaky mode. The theme music would start playing in my head ("secret agent man, secret agent man, they've given you a number and taken away your name...") and I would start thinking, *Act nonchalant. They can smell fear...* For all practical purposes, I was afraid every cop was waiting to get me. I would even slow down for people who, for some divisive reason, bought a car that looked like a police car (Crown Victorias, Mercury Marquis, and the like). Now I was slowing down for anyone and everyone who looked "cop-like." I needed to get insurance, but I was in graduate school and therefore my finances were more concerned with textbooks and food than insurance. I even went online, applied for insurance, but before I got to the "Check Out" page, I printed it out, so it looked like I had proof of insurance. I went from mild, law-abiding citizen, to full-blown deviant.

This mild paranoia went on for about a month and a half until I finally had enough of the nervousness and fear of random road-blocks. I went to the website of an insurance company and got insurance in all of about ten minutes. A month and a half of nervous driving traded away for ten minutes of just getting it right and doing what I was supposed to do.

I learned several things through this dodging-the-law experience. One is that I could definitely fake my way through it. One night in Hattiesburg, we went through a roadblock, I provided my little sheet that I printed off of an insurance company's website, and away I went. I didn't really need insurance, now did I?

The second thing I learned is that police have bigger problems than speeding within the city limits. Only highway patrolmen enjoy giving speeding tickets. I am not sure how fast one must go down Capital Street to get a ticket, but every time I drive through there (or on Bullard or Fortification), everybody is airing it out. I have passed numerous policemen and they never bat an eye when a car goes whizzing by.

So what about it? Why bother getting insurance if anyone can front his way out of a traffic stop and not worry about the police giving him a ticket? Why bother obeying a rule if there is no punishment involved? It's because there is an absence of peace. There is stress in the relationship that may rupture at any minute—and the stress is needless.

Every time I saw a cop I cringed because I knew I was not doing what was required. The way I treated the police and reacted towards the police is the same way many of us treat God. We fall behind, we don't do something we should, or we did something we shouldn't have and there we are acting nonchalant in the fourteenth pew back—not too toward the back or people may think I am hiding, but not too close to the front just in case I have to make a break for the exit doors.

God seeks to free us—he wants us to come to him uninhibited. While driving without insurance, anywhere I went, I went with a sense of dread that I would somehow be discovered. The same goes for us when we seek to join in worship—God wants us to right what is wrong before we seek to offer up praise and worship to him. Why? Because God wants us perfect before we come to him? I don't think so. I think it is because God wants us to enjoy him and not be consumed with guilt when we try to enter his presence. God wants us to have joy and freedom in Him—and if we come shackled to our mistakes, short-comings, broken-relationships, or sin, we will not fully understand how great his joy and freedom truly is.

So what do we do? Do we try to become perfect and until that day, sit alone and pine away with doubt and a great sense of dread? No, of course not. Should we try to impress God with an offering, so he will not notice our short-comings? No, of course not. Rather, we should follow his instructions in Micah 6:8: "And what, O Man, does God require of you? To love mercy, act justly and walk humbly with your God." If you find yourself at the altar and remember you have something against your brother, leave your offering and go make amends with your brother, then give your offering.[12] God wants us to be free—free from ourselves, free from guilt, and free to accept God's love and songs of praise as they shower down upon us.

gizmos and
Jesus

The other day I was cruising down the road listening to a local Christian radio station and the music was interrupted for an important news brief. The encouraging news that they had to offer was that a church in the Silicon Valley had built "the largest Christian Youth Ministry Center" on the West Coast. These days, that is quite an accomplishment, because it seems that the meek have lost out and the new trend for churches is "bigger is better." Just how much "bigger and better" was it? Well, some fourteen million dollars later, a brand-spanking-new 70,000 square-foot building now stands in San Jose—and it is equipped with the standards of evangelism: thirty X-Box and PS2 gaming stations, six pool tables, an eleven station e-Mac lab, iPod listening stations, a full-service café, an eighty-seat arena, and a 650-seat auditorium. If that wasn't enough, it seems that the children were not forgotten as well— they have their very own 12-foot artificial tree that is the home to a mechanical talking Macaw, a playroom with 3D wall mounted animals, indoor bounce houses, an eighteen-foot indoor slide, and a myriad of murals.

How did this happen? Evidently some youth minister had just finished reading his daily devotion at Bill's Funtime Arcade, walked past a Best Buy, and into a StarBucks to order his daily cup-of-Joe.

And then the epiphany came to him: to create the world's largest, gizmo-filled building to attract troubled teens.

What great passion and vision this youth minister must have possessed. Who cares that the church spent enough money to provide employment to 17,500 workers in Afghanistan for a year or enough money to sponsor 36,458 children through Compassion International? What really matters is that they can now keep kids entertained. Sure, it is hard to grow up without hope, mercy, and love, but no one can buy those at an electronics store. But before you despair, thank God we can buy computers online. Now these weary souls can develop their opposable thumbs as they slam dunk, throw passes, race cars, and shoot invading enemies all while sitting on holy ground. I am sure Jesus wishes he could come back now to join in on the fun, too—he could download the Sermon on the Mount on a nifty MP3 player, have a chat room for wannabe believers, and he could have his own talking bird that would spout off blessing after blessing.

The Technophobe, The Dirty Old Man, and The Fisherman.

Please don't misunderstand me—I am not some technophobe who thinks technology should not be used within the church. I am also not an Amish-Puritan mix who thinks technology should be flogged and/or condemned to hell. I am also not a paranoid type who thinks computers are going to rise and rush our livelihood closer to Armageddon.

In fact, the issue at stake isn't technology, but rather the use of resources in pursuit of the common goal of the church. Since the Bible does not give much in written word about the price of churches, the use of churches, how many should be built and where, church leaders take liberties in the creation of church buildings. The church errs on this point by claiming that there are not very specific guidelines and tries to fit the church building and its aims closer to our own culture, so it will be more appropriate for our "society." If one looks at the example of the temple in the church, one can see that it was made for one purpose—worship. The Jews would go to the synagogues to worship, and whether through sacrifice, song or study, they would worship.

The church today relies on its buildings for much more than worship. Often the church is hosting some civic dinner, political rally, or children's Halloween festival, or it is establishing a kindergarten or full-fledged school. These things are not inherently bad things—it is why they are used that is important. If they are used to bring people closer to God in worship, then use them liberally. If, however, the purpose of any thing or event at church is only for recruitment, then I think the church is in error. If a church invests in technology, such as a new computer system, PowerPoint programs, and a LCD projector to aid with the worship hour, that is great. It helps people worship. If the church purchases a PS2, a LCD projector, and a surround-sound system to attract the kids down the block to come to church, they are in serious error. In the Great Commission, Jesus did not recommend the church drive around in white panel vans with candy, trying to lure some innocent kid to the door like a dirty old man. He also didn't tell us to have lavish dinners, so the members of high society would think God was great and his place, the church, was the hippest place around. Rather Jesus went out to where the people were, shared with them, and got to know them. He went to them. If technology is used in the church, church leaders should be careful that the use of the technology or other "gizmos" is to be in the leading of worship, not for making the church more attractive. If the church relies on "baiting" the local populace to recruit new members, the church will soon find itself with apathetic members wishing to be entertained or members with a true desire to reach the lost that only know how to sit and wait.

Jesus wasn't just making a metaphor when he called Peter a "fisher of men." Fishermen must be proactive, not reactive. The fish will not drop by the fisherman's house and wait for him to grab his net–the fisherman must take up his net and head to where the fish are. Jesus chose fishermen to represent his method of outreach because he knew their methods would not change over time—even today, fishermen go out for days at a time to find their livelihood. Whether the catch is dismal or it is in great numbers, the method remains the same—go where the fish are and try to catch them.

lost in the
Woods

While at Ole Miss, I managed to stay on the five-year plan. My plan consisted of not having a plan until I found out I couldn't graduate and then make modifications. During this unplanned part of my academic career, I took cool classes like canoeing, backpacking, and part of an outdoor survival techniques class. Our teacher was from Puerto Rico, and at the beginning of each class, he would admit that he really didn't know what he was doing. He said that he initially wanted to be a basketball coach, but things didn't work out like he planned and now he was our teacher. He also told us that Puerto Rico didn't have many great wildernesses to get lost in, and the only hunting he knew of was when other people were hunted by the law. That was the fun part of the class. I had heard that in his navigation class, he got a large group of students lost, and he waded through a large swamp to go find help. Many of us signed up hoping for the prospect of having an equally entertaining educational experience.

Thomas, Shelley, Tori, and I all agreed to take the class together because we thought it would be much more interesting as a group. During our Backpacking class, he taught us how to set up a tent, what equipment was best and other things. In describing a down sleeping bag, he stated that it had "goose leaves" in it. Yes, the class was definitely entertaining. As time went on, we reached the end of the semester and had to go on a backpacking trip with our class which would be our "final exam." These were the rules:

1. No alcohol

2. No smoking

3. Bring a tent

4. Meet at the Turner Center at 5:00 p.m.

By the time the day of the final rolled around, only rule four survived. He told us he didn't care, but don't bring anything illegal. Our group of four agreed that this may be a very interesting outing with our classmates.

Two days before the campout, a Russian lady asked me to go pick up her husband from the airport at 11:55 p.m. on Friday. I agreed, knowing that I would have to leave the campout and then return. But that was okay with me. One day before the campout, Shelley, Thomas, and Tori all asked me if my tent was waterproof. "Of course," I told them. What tent isn't waterproof?

On the day of the campout, everything was going as planned—we met at the Turner Center and headed out to the campsite. We hiked through the woods as I carried our three-room family tent by bear-hugging it all the way. We set up the tent, chatted, played cards, and then it started to rain. At first, I told them that the walls of the tent felt wet because it was cold. Soon, I couldn't ignore the constant dripping into the tent. Shelley declared that this was the worst campout ever, and soon everyone crowded in the one room that was higher than the rest to stay out of the pooling water. I think they even disliked me more when I announced that I must leave my leaking tent and drive to Memphis. I grabbed my raincoat, flashlight, and headed out.

I went to the University Village Apartments, picked up one Russian lady, drove to the airport, picked up one Russian man, returned to the Village Apartments, and then back to the state wilderness area where we were camping. It all went without a hitch, and I was soon climbing out of my truck with my raincoat and flashlight to head back to the campsite at 2:00 a.m. I started hiking along the little stream and soon broke away from the stream to make it to the campsite. I soon came back to the same place by the little stream. I tried again. Once again, I found myself at the same area of the stream. Okay, I told myself, don't panic. I knew from 4-H and Webelos that I should not go nuts—that never helps unless you are in a boxing match. I tried again. Same place. I started to go nuts. I was completely lost in the woods, in a steady downpour, and I had no idea how to get back to the campsite. My leaking tent was now starting to seem very inviting. I made myself sit down against a pine tree and relax. I'll just stay here until morning and then it will be easy to find a way out. I'll be okay. As long as this tree doesn't get struck by lighting, I'll be okay… I'm going to die out here.

And then I heard it—a voice. I didn't know who it was or why they were out in the woods or if they were lost too—it didn't matter. I locked onto where I heard the voice and charged through the woods toward the sound. I am sure the other campers thought a bear or some deranged bull was charging through the woods at them because I ran through briars, undergrowth, privet hedge, and anything else without stopping. The only time I stopped was when I ran through a spider web and yanked it off of my face. Upon doing so, I felt a very large, warm spider crawl up into the palm of my hand and stop. I screamed like I never knew I could, starting flailing wildly, and ran with even more speed towards the sound. I tumbled out of the edge of the woods into an open field where all of our classmates and their tents were set up. Only five people gathered around smoldering coals were still up and their unrelenting stares told me that I had not stayed calm *and* I had gone nuts. But, I didn't care. I was home. I didn't have to worry about spending the night leaning against a tree. I made it home. Scratched, bleeding from briars, and with an intense case of the willies from the spider, I shook and itched all the way to my glorious, leaking tent. I had made it home.

It is hard to describe how one feels when truly lost. It isn't the same as taking a wrong turn on the interstate and ending up in the wrong place in town. It was the kind of lost where I had no clue where I was, and no one else knew where I was either. It was terrible, and it made me desperate.

That feeling—utter desperation—is what the psalmist talks about when he says he called out for God until his voice grew weary and his eyes failed. Psalm 69:3 says, "I am weary with my crying; my throat is parched; my eyes fail while I wait for my God." His voice grew weary and his eyes failed? Most of us have only had our voice grow weary after attending a sporting event and our eyes have only failed when we watched television too long. At church, how do we come seeking after God? Do we sing quietly and complacently, treating church as an obligation and not as a joyful, enriching part of a loving and divine relationship? I do. I find myself singing songs where I don't know the words or if I do know the words, my life isn't reflecting what they say and my spirit feels separated from them. But I sing anyway, lest others think I am somehow "off" or not spiritual enough to sing them.

The reality of this cold paradigm that I had created hit me when our church was singing the song "Breathe." This song's chorus says "and I'm desperate for you" and the next chorus states that "I'm lost without you." I started thinking about what I was saying and suddenly realized that I really didn't know what desperate means.

What was I thinking when I didn't pay attention to the words? Why didn't I fully engage into worship? Had I really forgotten that we all were lost and only saved through God's grace? The only way to keep away the complacency and coldness of heart in worship that slowly creeps in is to never forget where we came from—separated and hopeless—and to always remember who paid the ultimate price for us. If we grasp what we are and who God is, worship should gush forth out of us like an uncontrollable spring.

As soon as I remembered the time when I was lost in the woods, I started trying to connect the same feeling with my relationship with God. How different my relationship with God would be if I searched and searched, clambered and crawled through darkness, rain and fear—to seek out the safety and home that God offers. May I struggle and cry out until all of my strength is expended. May I spend all of my energy seeking God and his will rather than be buried in complacency and selfishness. If only I traded away what encumbers me from true devotion and yearned to see God's face in the land of the living. How different the world around me would become after it sees what true devotion is and how good God is.

black cats and
Bonnevilles

Growing up, we always had pet cats. Names ranged from Scat, Snowball, Tigger, Yoda, Pogo, Junk Mail, Briquette, Bitty Kitty, and Schizo. All of them had their own unique abilities and characteristics: Snowball was a great hunter, Tigger was lazy, Scat was the laziest, Yoda was the oldest, and Briquette was a jet black cat with the sharpest claws. Once, Briquette attacked our pastor when he sat talking with my father. He can definitely attest that the cat's claws were very sharp.

Briquette was also known for her disappearing. On occasion, Briquette would come up missing, but as cats do, she would often resurface a few days later, hanging out on the back porch crying out that everyone should have missed her and should come and feed her. Once, however, she came up missing for a little longer time than usual and my mother began to get worried. Not that the cat's being missing or my mother's worrying were anything new, but my mom was worried nonetheless. Her fears were relieved when she found the cat four days later. The only problem is that she found it while we were in the car line at Jefferson Middle School.

My brother was in eighth grade and I was in sixth. Mom heard a thump or a flop while going through the curves on the way to school and wanted to check on the sound as soon as we could stop.

While we were stopped, waiting for the cars ahead of us to unload, she proceeded to get out of the car, open the trunk, and extract a weak, hungry, and somewhat bewildered black cat. Upon finding the cat, she lifted it up in the air, so my brother and I could see it over the open trunk and exclaimed, "I found her!" As she climbed back in the '89 Bonneville, she exclaimed, "Ohh, she must have climbed in there when I was loading the groceries in the house. I didn't think to look for her when I shut the trunk."

My brother and I weren't feeling too sorry for the cat at the moment because we were too busy trying to figure out how to answer the inevitable question—"hey, did I see your mom pull a cat out of your trunk?" Junior high proved to be a difficult time in life where "being cool" never worked due to events like this.

In retrospect, I should have felt sorry for the cat—Briquette was just minding her business, saw something open and inviting and hopped in the trunk. I am sure if Briquette knew that she was going to be trapped in darkness without food or water for several days, thrown side to side as the car flew through our city's streets, she would have thought twice about the experiment. And it wasn't really the cat's fault. Well, part of it was—the cat actually leapt into the trunk—but the cat didn't know that the trunk was going to close on it—and the cat never would have had the chance to jump in the trunk if it wasn't left open.

Is it possible that the one who left the trunk open was responsible for Briquette's harrowing experience? Perhaps. Sometimes we, as a church, look the other way when it comes to responsibility. It is a very comforting thought to think that anyone who messed up bears the entire responsibility, but it isn't a very accurate thought. I am sure that the Israelites who wandered in the desert because of the ten who reported the land of Canaan could not be taken felt like the ten really messed things up. But what would have happened if the people, rather than listening to these ten's complaints, had trusted God and consequently sided with Joshua and Caleb? They could have changed things. "They could have…" means they had some responsibility.

Just as there is a corporate responsibility seen with the Israelites and Briquette, there is a corporate responsibility within our daily lives. When an ex-con who is trying to keep out of trouble walks by an empty car and sees a purse on the seat , temptation rears its ugly head. If the person who left the purse out would have not left it in plain view, perhaps the ex-con would not be tempted to break the window, take the purse, and run. Sounds extreme doesn't it? Who am I to say that other people can lead others astray or that other people can inhibit others' pursuit of Christ? Look to the words of Christ: "but whoever causes one of these little ones who believe in me to stumble, it would be better for him to have a heavy millstone hung around his neck, and to be drowned in the depth of the sea." Whoa. That's a little harsh. All I am trying to say is, "Don't leave your trunk open," or, "Please, carry your purse inside with you." If we, in our thoughtlessness, laziness, or craftiness, create a situation where a brother or sister can stumble, we "allowed" them to sin. And if they have sin in their lives, then their relationship with God is hindered. So, as you can see, God is definitely concerned with what we do and how that affects our brothers and sisters in Christ.

As a church, we need to be proactive with our walk and the walk of others—not to come across as puritans that cane people when they do wrong—but rather protect others through establishing and maintaining personal relationships. We need to hold our brothers and sisters accountable. We need to be there when they are struggling, to be the iron that sharpens iron. For if we, the church, aren't there to come to sinners and help them, no one will; and it is certain that a fallen world will not even think about rescuing those about to fall.

making fun of
God's Children

When I was in high school, I was part of a singing group called Solid Rock. From my voice-cracking, excruciatingly-high freshman year until my self-declaredly mature senior year, I sang with this group and we went to churches, community events, revivals and, mostly, prisons. To this day I am not sure how or why we managed to sing in almost every large prison in Louisiana, but we did. In these prisons, we met artists, musicians, pastors, and athletes. From Washington to Dixon to Hunt to Angola Federal, we sang to grateful crowds who all at one point in their lives made terrible mistakes.

We spent more time at one prison in particular, Angola Federal Penitentiary, because we would sing two concerts on one trip. While there, the guards would show us the old section of the prison, an electric chair no longer in use, different sections of the current prison, and the two areas where we would be singing. During my four visits to Angola, I learned a lot about prisons and even more about why I don't want to go to one; nevertheless, during my junior year, I also learned about myself.

We always were able to set up our equipment and do a sound check before the prisoners started coming in to grab a seat. We would go to the side and pray for the service and those present and then take our assigned positions. Our music minister, Brother Bernie O'Parker, liked to use jazzed-up music (well, jazzed-up compared to the music at our church) and the prisoners always seemed to enjoy the concerts more than our own church congregation. The prisoners would clap, stand up, shout, and this time in particular, they would dance. One man—who appeared to be in his sixties—was dancing with all he had. He was up and down each aisle and never seemed to stop. His dancing closely resembled how the Peanuts cartoon characters danced in *Charlie Brown's Christmas*, and his fervor in dancing made him almost seem mad.

In between songs and also during breaks, we would all snicker to each other about the little old man breaking it down. It seemed rather humorous because I had never seen anything like it, and his dancing was a little unorthodox (if, of course, there is "orthodox" dancing). We laughed to ourselves and enjoyed watching him dance for our entire concert. Our concerts would last at least an hour and a half, and he danced every bit of it without slowing down. As the concert came to a close, we switched to a hymn and started a time for the invitation. As with every concert in a prison for men, the girls stayed on stage and sang and we "men" walked down front for the invitation. Before the girls were able to sing softly through the first verse of "I Will Follow Jesus," the old man stood up and walked down the aisle towards us. He came up to me, hugged me, and uttered in broken speech something that I will never forget: "I don't have my tongue, so I can't sing. I dance." He smiled at me, thanked me for our group coming and went to the others to thank them as well. Twenty plus years later, the memory of that event is still crystal clear. My chest tightens and tears come to my eyes when I remember how judgmental I was and how my shallowness blinded me from seeing one of God's children. I believe that when God saw him, he saw a man fully emptied of himself, giving himself in a genuine act of worship. Now when I think of that old man, I look upon him with awe; I see someone who I seldom am—one who could express his worship to Christ without being concerned about what others think and who could give all he had in every way he could.

the turtle, the helicopter,
and the Gravel Road

I love bike riding. In fact, it probably qualifies as my favorite sport. This is true because I hate running and I am an introvert. These two personal preferences have helped elevate biking to "favorite" status only to be challenged by kayaking or sailing on occasion.

While living in Jackson, I would ride my bike from the duplex I lived in towards the Natural Science Museum. Then I would cycle down Lakeland (which is close to suicidal these days), and then I would turn in towards Mayes Lake. Where I turned off usually would change depending on how far I made it before having to swerve off the road to avoid traffic.

Mayes Lake was a nice, peaceful ride that is somewhat secluded despite the metropolis that has engulfed it on every side. The only setback about the ride was that it was a gravel road that got quite dusty during the summer. I usually didn't care about riding on gravel roads, but I had loaned out my hybrid bike and was left with only a road bike. This bike would work on the gravel road, but required a lot of attention to keep from flopping over while riding towards the lake. It just so happened that as I was riding on the gravel road, I saw an enormous turtle crossing the road. I thought it would make a great addition to our house as an official mascot and scooped it up. As I road on further, I had to hold the turtle away from me because it had since overcome its shyness and was now trying its best to bite me. I carried it a while with my left hand, but my left arm soon tired and I swapped hands. Now as I careened down the road, it didn't really dawn on me that I could only grab my front brake because my right hand was holding a terrapin rather than the rear brake lever.

I was moseying along when I heard a helicopter approaching and glanced upward to see where it was. If you know anything about me, you know I have an obsession with rotary aircrafts and amphibious vehicles. The helicopter, fitting into one of these categories, soon demanded my utmost attention as I pedaled on. The only problem about looking for helicopters, especially when riding a bike on a gravel road while holding a turtle elevated away from you, is that it is very easy to wreck. And this I did. I came on a turn in the road and turned too sharply when I realized I was missing my turn. My actions soon had me falling turtle first to the right, so I instinctively grabbed the brake. Since only my left hand was available for the job, my front tire locked up, wheel yanked sideways, and I went headfirst and towards the left into the gravel. I managed not to drop the turtle, but my trying to save the turtle left no other hands to soften the fall, so I landed on my back with a *whump*. Although the wind was knocked out of me, I leapt up in case there were any other bystanders to witness my klutzy wipeout. As I glanced around, I could feel the turtle wiggling fervently in an effort to declare that it had had enough adventure for the day. In defeat, I laid the turtle in the ditch and watched in envy as he crawled towards the water with a very low center of gravity.

With the helicopter slipping out of sight beyond the tree line and the turtle rustling through the undergrowth, quickly walking away from its incompetent kidnapper, I chuckled to myself and shook my head at my misadventure. "Of course I was going to wreck," I mused. "I took my eyes off of where I was going, I was holding onto something that was not needed, and I was on the wrong type of path for my bicycle." Rather than being upset that I fell down, I should have been amazed that I made it as far as I did and that I didn't see the inevitable crash coming.

What happened to me has actually happened several times before—not specifically with a turtle and a helicopter—but with many other things. If you think about it, I am sure you have found yourself in a similar predicament. Have you ever agreed to do something and then found out it was too much? Have you ever lost sight of what you were trying to do and found yourself off course or down and out? It happens to all of us. It even happened to the disciples. They were following Jesus and carried their pride along. How else do people tell the Son of God that they want reserved seats when they get to heaven? That takes audacity. Or tell little children to go away because they would bother Jesus? They were holding onto something that they didn't need and as a result lost sight of what was right in front of them. And Jesus's reply? That they do not need to look out for number one, but to seek to be the lowest—to be the servant of servants. They need to be like children when they come to God because "the kingdom of Heaven is to such as the children."[13]

So what are you holding onto? Part of our culture is to hold onto things and to do a lot. I am not sure of it, but I believe that Americans created the word "multitasking." We live in a fast-paced culture that makes us believe that texting people, planning business meetings, and spending time with the kids can all be done while driving down a busy interstate. Jesus probably wouldn't have had a planner or a cell phone because he wouldn't have needed them; he only had one goal. And beyond that goal, everything else just followed in the wake of it. Imagine how peaceful that would be? Keep this goal number one and don't worry about the rest. For me on my bike, it would have been ride down the road and don't worry about flying machines or reptiles. Jesus said it pretty simply: "Seek first His kingdom and His righteousness, and all these things will be added to you." Hmm. Sounds pretty easy doesn't it? And if you are like me, you probably think you have this figured out.

"I'll keep God number one. Family number two. Job number three. Country... number four? Maybe I'll have to put that in between number two and three. Yard work definitely somewhere near number seventy-three. Reaching out to the neighbors? That probably should be top ten so I can remain pious. Football season. Uh-oh—maybe bump it up to number two for a little while and merge family, neighbors, and football into one by watching the game after a barbeque. Insurance, bills, soccer tryouts, shopping, hiking, photography, church, choir—this is starting to get too much…" Next thing you know, you are going to start feeling bad for rearranging the number system because the bridge club on Thursdays feels like it comes before the children, and on Wednesday you just don't have any time because of choir practice, Wednesday night church, soccer, and hospital visitation. Meanwhile, Jesus just sits on the sidelines feeling worried for your sanity as you blitz back and forth. He desperately wants you to hear and understand what he said: "Seek ye first the kingdom of God and the rest will be given to you."

In Jesus's paradigm there was no list, no top ten, and no graph to show just how priorities may shift depending on what time he woke up that morning and whether or not he had the big cup of coffee or just got stuck in traffic. He just had a number one. That is why he didn't declare that Peter would sit in the fourth chair on the left and John second from the right when the disciples wanted to know about their reserved seats in Heaven. That thought probably never crossed Jesus' mind. That is also why he didn't have to worry about what would happen when they asked him if he was the Son of God. It was automatic—"You will see the son of man descend…" If family, life, or the pursuit of happiness was anywhere on his list, the answer would not have been so easy. But they were nowhere to be found. And when there is only one choice, then that is the easy answer. Give glory to God. What will you do? Give glory to God. What will happen to your friends? Give glory to God. This week your boss is going nuts and may fire all of us! Give glory to God. You feel down and out because your marriage is a little rocky and you feel like giving up… Give glory to God. Why? Not to give thanks for good or bad things, but to declare that God is all you need and if you have God everything else will work out because with God all things are possible.

One last example is seen in hapless Peter trying to walk on the water. There is no telling how many thousands of sermons have been preached about Peter taking his eyes off Jesus and focusing upon the waves. Peter is now our "disciple" example of losing focus because he sunk and Jesus had to reach for him. But Peter—just like us—probably had a few good reasons to look to the waves. For a pastor 2,000 years later to preach about not looking at the waves is a lot easier to say from behind a pulpit than it was for Peter placing his feet down on the surface of the sea. It isn't easy—whether it is how we were raised, how we naturally worry, or how we just can't focus for more than two minutes—we take our eyes off what should be our all in all. Many of us know how Peter felt as he was sinking and feel down because of our failures, but take heart—Peter may have lost his focus while walking on the waves, but he was the only one to step out of the boat that day.

God's Touch

We say so many things about God, but we really don't understand the significance of our utterances. We say God is love, God is omnipotent, and God is good. We have an idea of what love is and should be, and we attempt to love each other.

Love between two people is easier to comprehend than the love that God showers down on a creation that rebelled against Him. I have heard many people try to explain God's love by telling an example of a king who came and died for slaves, but that is not as deep or profound as God's love. The best way to provide insight into the great, wondrous love of God is to imagine what it is like to love perfectly the imperfect. If you were the creator, what would you do if your pride and joy, your precious creation, said to you that there is more to life than you and told you that it no longer has a need for you? I am willing to guess that you would disassemble your creation the way a child smashes a Lego creation when the newness wears off. After your creation was reduced to its smallest parts, you would start over and make a more respectful, more loving, and more loyal creation. But thankfully, God is different.

In my attempts to understand God and his attempts to help me understand his character, I often find myself struggling to grasp even the smallest facet of God's perfect qualities. Why? Because everything God is, I am not. God is holy; I am unholy. God is perfect; I am imperfect. The list goes on and on. I find more comfort than discomfort in the fact that God and I are not alike. One thing on this list of who and what God is, is his willingness to touch. I have come to marvel at God's eagerness to touch and the change that comes with God's touch.

God designed us to touch. Touch helps bring moments to a more intimate level and gives a physical representation of what words espouse. Just observe a reunion at any given airport. Amidst tears and squeals of joy, you see lovers, mothers and daughters, husbands and wives enraptured by the tightest hug—this touch gives tangible evidence for their longings for each other. If anyone or anything is cognizant of this part of the human psyche, it is God—for God has made us in his image.

Have you ever thought about Jesus longing to be held? If we long for a hug after the coffee spilled on our suit, the kids were late to school, and we were given a speeding ticket en route to a meeting for which we were already late, why wouldn't Jesus need a hug after people refused to love him or revere him after he had given his all? I believe that is one of the reasons that Jesus' anointing by the "sinful woman" had such an impact on him and those around him. This woman who needed Jesus more than the others present was also the only one who saw Jesus' own needs.[14] Thousands thronged to get in God's welfare line for food and healing, but few came to God offering their love and their touch. In the scriptures people rarely reached out to Jesus, although it was very common to read about Jesus reaching out to them. Do not be misled—it is not because Jesus did not need others to reach for him; to give him a helping hand. Rather it is in our human condition that we seek after our own needs before others and would rather take than give—even when the one we see before us is perfect. This self-serving lifestyle is not only seen in the Bible, but even our own prayers echo this behavior. We rarely bless God for who he is, but we never fail to ask for God's blessings.

Jesus's touching people is all the more remarkable because he did not have to touch anyone to help them. God's love is great because it is perfect. God's love is greater because it was given by his own volition. God could have been a cold deity that forced us into an automaton state of existence. Rather, God chose to love us despite our inconsistencies and divided loyalties. Healing the sick, he did not have to touch them.

There are a few instances in which Jesus heals people without touching them, but just by his command. No abracadabra or slap upon the forehead; nothing one would anticipate seeing on television. Just his word was present. Jesus's commands carried the power of God and the power of God yielded the healing. When Jesus healed the man with the shriveled hand,[15] Jesus told him to stretch out his hand—and the man was healed. Again when a Roman centurion requested that Jesus heal his servant, the centurion knew that Jesus's voice alone would yield healing.[16] And it did.

If Jesus did not need to touch the sick to heal them, why did he do so? Is it because he enjoyed becoming unclean according to Jewish law? Is it that he wanted to touch diseased, crippled, and dying bodies? No, he touched people because he understood touch, and he understood what it was like to be human. He understood what it was like to be tired and need a helping hand. He knew what it was like to be afraid and need to be reassured. He knew what it was like to experience loss and need an empathetic caress. Not only did Jesus understand these things firsthand, he knew people experienced it because he knew their inmost being.[17] Who can understand better than the Creator? Jesus understood humanity and that is the reason he breached religious walls of insincerity to heal the unwanted, the used, and the broken.

Touching the sick was a larger task in Biblical times than it is today. One only needs to look at the innumerable laws of the time to understand this was no small endeavor. Lepers were ostracized from the community. If anyone approached them for any reason, the law required them to cry out in a loud voice saying they were "unclean." And if anyone touched them, they would become unclean. Unclean? What is "unclean"? Jesus came to say that what was "unclean" was loveable and in need of a Savior.

Countless times, Jesus confronted the religious leaders in regard to their innumerable laws. Jesus tried to get them to realize that it was not the outside of the cup that was important, but what was on inside that counted.[18] Jesus saw the inside of the "cup" for these people.[19] Broken. Lonely. Ashamed. For these reasons Jesus's heart reacted with compassion when he saw the multitudes. They were "sheep without a shepherd" and he came to be that shepherd.[20] Jesus also knew that in God's eyes, all people were unclean. What the Sadducees and Pharisees did not understand is that if all the "unclean" were required to call out in a loud voice, the earth would be filled with a cacophony of screams: "Embezzler!" "Holier-Than-Thou!" "Cheater!" "Murderer!" "Lustful!" "Speeder!" "I-fudged-on-my-tax-forms!" "Glutton!" "Prideful!" The cries would be endless. But Jesus did not need to hear the cries of the hurt—he knew that all were hurting and he came to heal them. Jesus touched these hurting individuals with healing, rescuing, and blessing.

The recorded miracles of Jesus healing the sick are amazing. Jesus healed the lame and raised the dead. He took all that a broken world can offer and fixed it, healed it, and perfected it. When Jesus healed a man with leprosy, he reached out and touched him. The law, for years, had made this man unable to draw close to God, so God drew near to him, touching him, healing him, and making him whole.

Shortly after healing the man with leprosy, Jesus reached for Peter's mother-in-law's hand, healing her of a fever.[21] Later in the book of Matthew, Jesus is telling a crowd that the funeral is all a mistake because the deceased child is just sleeping.[22] I am sure the crowd around Jesus was laughing, muttering under their breaths that the "idiot from Nazareth has lost his mind." Meanwhile a little girl in the presence of God was being told that she was going back to see her mother again. Jesus grabbed the girl's hand and she got up. Something so simple, yet so amazing.

In rescuing Peter, the Bible states that Jesus "caught" Peter.[23] I had always imagined Jesus' reaching down with an outstretched hand grasping Peter's arm in a pious act of divinity. But the word "caught" gives a different impression. This image is akin to a fire-fighter carrying a child from a fire—cradling the child in his arms. Jesus could have shouted to the sea to stop, and it would have spit Peter out like a cork in a champagne bottle. Jesus's love, however, reacted to the situation, and here is Jesus holding a scared, sopping wet, unbelieving Peter. We see God no longer as a detached deity, but close, soaking wet, holding Peter as a mother holds a precious child, loving and instructing Peter. Reaffirmed in the arms of his Savior, Peter held this Jesus in a new light—and a God that didn't just give instruction, but one that would stoop down to bear his fear, his burdens, and his lack of faith. That is a God of wonder.

The last example of God's touch is his touch of blessing. People wanted to bring their children to Jesus.[24] This is significant on many levels. Not many people have enough trust to hand their children over to a stranger, especially not to someone who has no home. Can you imagine seeing your neighbor taking his newborn to the local soup kitchen and handing the child over for a vagrant to hold? Hmm. And yet something about this mysterious Jesus led people to him—to have him hold them, bless them, love them. Jesus told them to bring their children to him—he loved them and saw in them a genuine worth and faith—and a promise for better tomorrows.[25]

If we understand that Jesus did not need to heal people—he is God and can choose to do as he likes—and even if he chose to heal people, we know He did not have to touch them, then we would be in awe of who God truly is.

Know that there is a God in heaven that loves you. He knows your name and wants to hold you. God in the flesh wants to hold your hand. Why? Think about it. You know the feeling of being separated from the one you love. Whether it is a business trip, sickness, or something more permanent—death—to miss one that you love is a powerful feeling that wrenches one's soul. Imagine if the one whom you loved this much was your own creation and you loved them with a love that was so great and perfect, yet you were misunderstood by everyone around. Not only is the love perfect, the separation has been for thousands of years. The heart-wrenching feeling that has been pent up now comes gushing forth as a dam breaking under pressure. God's love came in the form of his own: Jesus Christ. And he wanted to hold their hands.

shooting
the Postman

When my parents lived in Columbia's city limits, my greatest joy was to ride my little BMX bike all over the neighborhoods. My brother and I would strike out to all sorts of destinations, especially an arcade a few miles away. No one our age lived in our neighborhood, so we found countless shortcuts through other people's yards to zip over to friends' homes in other neighborhoods. One of our favorite shortcuts went through an elderly man's terraced backyard which seemed like a perfect yard of ramps.

One day I rode my bike down from the Orchard Drive subdivision where we lived into the Ridgewood subdivision. A friend of mine, Chris, lived there and he always was up to something. Chris's parents bought him absolutely everything, and because of their personal efforts in driving the local economy, we all thought Chris was cool. He had every Transformer ever made and even had a jet ski—which was really cool even though we really didn't know what that was. Another one of his possessions was his bike (his was much better than mine) and we would sometimes go riding together. With riding and a little mischief in mind, I rode toward his house. As I approached his house, I noticed that he was hiding in the bushes and was wearing a Spiderman ski mask. He often wore his ski mask while playing soccer, which led people to believe he was a little off his rocker, but I knew deep down he was really cool. As I got even closer, I noticed he had a pellet rifle cradled in his lap. As an elementary school kid, that looked like a lot of fun, and I rode over to him to ask what was going on.

"Shh. Get down. He is coming in a few minutes," Chris said in a hushed tone. To hear such a hushed tone coming from behind a Spiderman ski mask made him seem a little psychotic, but I decided to play along. I dove in the bushes behind him and asked who "he" was, hoping that "he" somehow personified a squirrel. Chris peered around, glanced back at me, and said, "The mailman." Of course, I thought. What an easy target. The mailman came at about the same time every day and was really easy to identify. It was sort of like going deer hunting after putting up surveillance cameras and baiting a field. Plus, it probably wasn't going to get us into too much trouble because he was only going to shoot him with a pellet rifle. That sounded like real fun, so I decided to hang out in the bushes with Chris.

We sat in the bushes for a good half hour with Chris occasionally checking his sights and leaning out of the bushes to peer around. In school, most of our teachers accused us of having ADHD, but out in the yard, hiding in the bushes, we sat still as the minutes slowly crept by. After sitting in suspense for over an hour, I had already figured out what I was going to tell mom when she was notified (by the mailman, Chris's mom, or the police). I was going to tell her that I wasn't the one who pulled the trigger and I really didn't know he was going to shoot the mailman. As I was mulling over what I was going to do after we shot the mailman, a little white Jeep rounded the corner in the distance and started its stop-and-go motion from mailbox to mailbox.

"Here he comes," Chris motioned down the street. At that he checked to make sure he had a pellet loaded in the barrel and eased the barrel out towards his mailbox.

Up until that point, I planned to stay and witness the entire event because I thought it would be interesting and make a great story to tell. But when the moment came, I inexplicably crawled out of the bushes, backing away from Chris as quietly as I could, grabbed my bike, and took off. I didn't say anything as I left, mainly because I was afraid Chris might have shot me since I possibly ruined his surprise attack. I am not sure what made me leave, but perhaps it was a little common sense, a little realization of the punishment to come, and a little knowing that it was wrong to ambush the poor postman. Whatever happened afterward, I never asked or brought it up again. I left behind what we both thought would be fun and exciting—I left it without speaking and without any explanation. I just left.

Of my reasons for leaving, they all gravitated toward one thing: I knew it was wrong. It is not that I didn't want to stay and watch—there were thousands of excuses I could give about how it would be exciting, I never had done it before, and it really wasn't me that started it, and it was Chris' idea, not mine. Despite all of my reasons for hanging around and experiencing the shooting of the postman, I knew it was wrong. Not that my mom sat me down and started this long conversation about the mailman and the pellets and why it is wrong to shoot people with a pellet gun. She just taught us what was right and what was wrong by a standard that God set; a standard that put others before us, even when we didn't want to. The standard was rigid, not flexible.

Although the circumstances differed greatly from my experience, Joseph found himself in a situation that forced him to choose between what would be "new and exciting" or what was right. Joseph was far from home, second in command, and his boss was nowhere around. His boss's wife, who no doubt was very attractive, came to him day in and day out to ask him to sleep with her. If Joseph had used a value system that the world accepts as good, he would have had a hard time running away. He could rationalize: "Well, it wasn't my idea. It was hers. I am far from home, and mom and dad won't find out. Who cares what my brothers think—they sold me. Perhaps her husband just isn't 'right' for her. You know it is important to be satisfied in a relationship—I learned that from a talk show. Plus, there aren't anything like DNA testing or polygraphs, so I am pretty sure I could get away with it. I deserve a break—I have been Mr. Goody-Two-Shoes, and now I am going to sow some wild oats. She is the one asking for it..."

The list goes on and on. Anyone can justify anything if he does not have a standard. It is easy. Just look at history for the example. Try to think of the worst, most unimaginable atrocity that no one justified. You can't think of it because it doesn't exist. For every terrible thing that happened during our lifetimes or in the Old and New Testaments, people justified it. Not only one person, but many people justified it. And that is what happens in the absence of absolute good.

As Christians, we have an absolute. Christ did not describe himself as one who was pointing to the way, but that he was "the Way." Some days that is a tough line to follow, but know that struggles are expected. When you find yourself up against the wall, tempted beyond what you think you can handle, remember these words: "No temptation has overcome you but such as is common to man; and God is faithful, who will not allow you to be tempted beyond what you are able, but with the temptation will provide the way of escape also, so that you will be able to endure it."[26]

Also, when found in a position where you are tempted, you must have something to run to—you can't just run aimlessly away because you probably will run into some other type of trouble. Paul instructed Timothy to stay away from evil and to "pursue righteousness, godliness, faith, love, perseverance and gentleness."[27]

When you find temptation at your elbow, whether it is when you are out of town or out with old friends or up late surfing the internet, know that you have help in your struggle. You have a Savior that understands that temptation is tough—so tough that sometimes it is alright just to run away.

the good thing about
Darkness and Light

I had just moved into my new apartment and my roommate and I were digging through some of my junk trying to get organized. It was getting a little warm, so I cut on the air conditioner and resumed unpacking. Everything was going well, but suddenly, the power went off. My first thought was that I didn't pay the power bill, but I knew that shouldn't have anything to do with it—mainly because I didn't cut the power on in the first place; we were just using it while it was under our landlord's name. I was supposed to switch it over on Tuesday since today (Monday) was a holiday. Well, the power company apparently did not observe holidays, and now it was exceptionally dark. Even outside it was pitch black. My roommate exclaimed that all of the power in the city had gone off and ran to his room to retrieve a flashlight. If reincarnation actually existed, my roommate would come back as a golden retriever. Nothing gets him down—including a blackout. He was elated to have an opportunity to show how prepared he was, and he was soon walking around making the beam of his flashlight dance around the walls of our living room. He and I then went out to my truck to dig around for my flashlight. After finding it, we went outside and watched our neighbors emerge from their houses wielding candles, flashlights, or cell phones (those things have multiple uses).

We were soon informed that a cat cashed in its ninth life by leaping into a power relay station and that the power may be off for a while. Thirty minutes later, I became bored and tired of wielding my huge flashlight, which is the kind that doubles as a baseball bat in case one needs to fend off raiding parties at midnight. I ducked inside, grimaced at the sight of our AC sitting idle, and headed back to my room. I sat down and tried to work by the light of my flashlight, but this proved to be cumbersome. After a while, I capitulated in my battle against the darkness and decided to sleep. That seemed the apt thing to do since it was the easiest, so I flopped down on my bed, shined my flashlight at the ceiling while checking out how dirty it was (we just moved in, so it wasn't my dirt), and cut off my flashlight. And there it was. My ceiling looked like the Milky Way. I cut the flashlight back on, expecting to see glow-in-the-dark stickers but saw none. I cut off the flashlight. More little "stars" appeared where my flashlight had been. Cool. In the dark, my mind first pondered why someone would paint over glow-in-the-dark stars, but then decided that it must be glow-in-the-dark paint. After that debate, I looked at the stars and tried to figure out if they spelled something or if the stars were arbitrarily thrown upon the ceiling. No, definitely randomly placed.

Seeing the stars reminded me of the time I moved into the dorm my freshman year in college and cut the lights off the first night away from home. There was something in glow-in-the-dark paint there as well, but it was some devil-looking creature exclaiming, "I'm coming to get you, Judd." That was a somewhat more frightening discovery than the stars. I didn't want to remember much more of my freshman year in college, especially the time I lost my scholarship, so I started daydreaming while staring at the new-found stars.

My mind drifted over to the last phone call I had and how I was soon going to go to a music concert. Then I started daydreaming about what it would be like to play the guitar and sing in front of a crowd of several hundred people. I soon was day-dreaming about strumming my guitar and doing one of those long intros that nobody really likes except the guitarist because he really thinks it is cool. Soon I was introducing my songs, playing songs, and personifying my guitar—I couldn't think of a good name, so I kept referring to my guitar as "her." From there my mind wandered on to how B.B. King named his guitar "Lucille" and was audibly muttering how it had something to do with two men fighting over a girl named Lucille and how B.B. King had to rescue his guitar from the bar when it caught on fire. Then my mind drifted on to playing the guitar again, but this time with pyrotechnics shooting off everywhere and me jumping around the stage like Van Halen.

Then something happened that interrupted my daydream and really confused me: the ceiling exploded into light. The ceiling erupted into light so suddenly and brightly that my eyes, accustomed to dark, couldn't focus on anything. Slowly my rods and cones finished wrestling with themselves, and I could see a little of the supernova going on in the ceiling. I was a little discombobulated, but as I could hear the hum of the air conditioner in the other room I realized that I had been staring directly where my light fixture was when the power came on. Getting up, trying to blink away the bright spots burned into my vision, I started unpacking again. Now as I sorted through my belongings, I pondered what I learned from the glow-in-the-dark stars in my room.

The power outage was in no way an invited event—I really do enjoy having an air conditioner, lights, a running computer, etc. But if it weren't for the power outage, I would have never noticed the stars above me. The uninvited darkness inadvertently revealed the light. The same situation is in the world—the darkness tries so hard to conceal the light, but it actually makes the light that God gives seem even brighter.

Jesus knew what he was talking about when he said that he was the light—not only can you see more in the light, but light gives life, gives warmth, and without it we could not exist. This world can be quite the antithesis of light—rather than giving clarity, the world around us tries to obfuscate the truth by using the darkness that naturally comes. Sometimes the darkness comes around us and sometimes it enters us when we find ourselves away from the Light.

Peter no doubt felt that way. Before his denial, he knew God was powerful—Jesus healed countless people, including Peter's own mother-in-law. He knew that God could provide—he saw five thousand or more people receive more than they could eat from a little boy's lunch. He knew that God controlled creation—Peter saw that while walking on the water. He even saw God forgive people who were steeped in sin—he saw Christ forgive the woman caught in adultery. But how about God's forgiveness to those who had put their hands to the plow and turned back? What about Peter, who tried so hard and fell even harder? Peter found the depths of God's love and forgiveness when the lights went out. When Peter was at the lowest point in his devotion to God, that was when Christ came to him and showed him what true love really was.[28] Three times Christ commanded a broken-down Peter to not despair and to feed His sheep.

Paul saw the light of God both literally and figuratively on the road to Damascus. Countless stories exist in the Bible about people, just like us, who took their eyes off of the light or purposely shut the light out—and in doing so, found the light even brighter. Despite their waywardness, God called to welcome them back into fellowship.

As for me, I thought I was alright—I grew up in church and had a New Testament in my back pocket wherever I went. It was only when I found myself in college, away from all of the superficial supports that I had depended on for so long, that I found myself in the dark. You may find yourself in a similar position where you know only darkness—the kind of darkness that isn't only seen but felt. But take courage; it is in the dark where we realize how great the light truly is.

awe and the
Mystery of Elevators

When I was little, I was mystified with the elevator at our church. It was mysterious because my parents would not let me get near it (I had a propensity for breaking things), only old people used it and it had its own little room that you entered before you could enter the elevator. The little room gave it an eerie feel because it was set up identically to the visitation room that the church used during funerals—so I associated the whole thing with being old or dying.

During Royal Ambassadors, we would often look at the elevator and dare each other to ride it. We were awed by it; we even feared it. Only older people entered it, so we thought it must be an adult thing—and being eight years old, the adult world was a vast mystery to us. So one night, we decided that we needed to find out exactly what the elevator did and where it would take us. Countless times, we would make it into the elevator, but when the doors would start to shut, we would abandon ship before the doors could completely close. Once, one of our group of explorers hit the big red "stop" button out of fear; that set off an alarm and we ran and ran and ran from the accursed beast until we could run no more.

Then the day came that I braved the elevator and let the doors shut. Actually I did not brave it. We were daring each other to wait until the doors started to shut, and I was too slow to exit the elevator. And then nothing happened. That was not funny at all. I tried to pry the doors open, but nothing. I tried and tried to jam my little fingers in the crack between the doors, but to no avail. I looked at the nondescript, elevator walls and wondered how people got in the elevator and then disappeared. I glanced over to the control panel and saw a box for a telephone and four buttons: one with arrows going in, one with arrows going out, one with the letter "A" and one with the letter "B." Just when I thought I was on the verge of understanding elevators, I was now more confused. The controls seemed to be more for a garbage compactor than a device for transport.

While I was staring at the buttons, the doors opened. My friends stared back at me in amazement, shocked that I was still in the elevator. One of them mashed the button to see if I had disappeared since they didn't hear any whirring noise after I entered. Upon the doors opening, I exited not wanting to be trapped in that bewildering box.

We pondered why I didn't go anywhere and thought that we couldn't use it because of our age—kind of like the limits at roller coasters. That must be why our parents told us not to get in it, we reasoned. What was the point of trying if we were too young? After our anticlimactic experiment, we postponed our discoveries for later and ran down the hall to another adventure.

A week later, we decided that we would go in and not leave until something happened. The following Wednesday night, I showed up with a flashlight jammed in my pants pocket, a pocket-knife in my jacket pocket, and some matches. One of the other guys always carried a roll of duct tape and some string in his pockets. We pooled our supplies and felt like we were ready to explore the elevator. Two of us climbed on the elevator and the others hid in the elevator room and waited. The two of us who boarded the elevator stood in the center just in case something came out of the walls, and we waited. The doors shut and we were enclosed in silence. While standing in silence, none of us spoke out of fear we would miss some sound that would warn us of danger. I looked around for something to press to make the machine move—since the building

I was in was only two stories, there were not many options to query, so I pressed "A." That seemed the safest option, but all that did was open the doors. After repeating the "press 'A'" experiment to make sure the results would turn out the same, I then pressed "B." When I depressed the bold-faced "B," the doors slid shut and the extra-large refrigerator-sized box lurched upward. As it ground to a halt, the doors opened into another room that I had not seen before. We were a little concerned because the room that it opened up to was very similar to the one we left, but the flowers were different and there was a small table on the far wall that wasn't in the other room. This new room was also not as well lit, but most importantly, our friends had disappeared. Well, at least the two of us were safe, so we slowly crept out of the room into a darkened hall where we could vaguely hear singing. We slowly walked down the hallway, making note of any potential hiding places if our parents, our R.A. leader, or any other adult happened to come in looking for us. At the end of the hall, I peered through the crack of the doors in front of me and could see people in robes singing. That meant the choir room, which meant the choir, which meant my mom was in the room which probably meant I was going to be in trouble.

Although our success was dampened by the fact that our moms saw us walk nonchalantly by the choir room entrance, we were nonetheless greeted like great explorers by the rest of our group at the bottom of the stairwell. One mystery down, millions more to go.

When I was little, I held many things in awe—elevators, helicopters, the "bugman" (the guy who would drive through our neighborhood and fog the mosquitoes), planes, turtles, hovercrafts, and our neighbor who was rumored to have been arrested for possessing a bazooka. I can also add to the list anything that my parents forbade me to touch, play with, taste, or go near. There is something about restrictions that peak curiosity levels.

What fascinated me when I was younger, however, is not what fascinates me now. With human nature, we have a tendency to become infatuated with something or another, but that soon passes as the newness wears off. As a result, we move from one thing to another, seeking something more interesting, something more modern, or just something more fun. Elevators are no longer mystical or forbidden. If anything, they are too slow or weird because people seem to all know elevator etiquette without ever discussing it. Planes used to amaze me, but now they are everyday things that I see in the sky (I live near an airport) and if anything they scare me more than amuse me.

In an effort to explain awe and how one comes to have it, I turned to an online dictionary to define it. Dictionary.com defines awe as *an overwhelming feeling of reverence, admiration, fear, etc., produced by that which is grand, sublime, extremely powerful, or the like.* The examples given use awe in the fragments: *in awe of God* and *in awe of great political figures*[29]. Awe of the elevator was found in its mystery and how we didn't really understand how it worked. As children, we truly revered it as an amazing machine. An awe of God is similar in that it is finding amazement in His mystery and greatness. Inevitably, to have awe for someone or something begins with the realization that the someone or something is greater than we are. Awe, mystery, and greatness are all intertwined because without greatness or mystery, there would be no awe.

As for my walk with Christ—I can identify specific times when I saw God with true awe. I vividly remember the first night I accepted Christ as my Lord and Savior. I can remember crying tears that came out of nowhere and how it felt like a million pounds were taken off my chest as I made the decision to drop my desires and cling to the cross. I remember how Bible studies exploded off the page and how I had a thirst, a hunger, to know more about the One I swore to follow.

Could you imagine how different life would be if our awe didn't wane over time? Life would be more interesting, more electrified, but others would probably think we were crazy. Imagine standing next to someone waiting for the elevator and she turns around and says, "This is going to be so cool. This thing just shows up, opens its doors, and takes us up, up and away and we don't even have to walk!" You would probably excuse yourself and look for an elevator more likely to have passengers that will just quietly stare at the numbers above the door than choose to cram into the cramped confines of an elevator with a nutcase. Sure that example is a little extreme, but transfer that principle to worship. How would our lives be changed if we walked into church and found ourselves standing next to someone who greeted us by saying, "This is going to be so great. We get to come once again into the presence of an almighty God that loves us so much and he allows us to come and praise Him. I can't wait. Aren't you excited?" That would leave us with a choice to make—to think the person is some religious whacko or to agree that God is indeed awesome. If we came together in worship with true awe of God, we would no doubt be changed and we would change those around us.

The Psalmists in the Bible often spoke of awe and how great God is. In Psalm 22:23, 33:8, and 65:8, the psalmists proclaim that people should stand in awe of God. [30] Not to just have awe, but to react to it. Awe is an emotion that demands a response. The automatic response of catching a glimpse of an amazing God is to stand in awe, fear, and reverence. What a picture of true awe. In the book of Acts, it states that "Everyone kept feeling a sense of awe; and many wonders and signs were taking place through the apostles."[31] How amazing it is when God is moving among us and through us. Lastly, in Hebrews, the writer states that "since we receive a kingdom which cannot be shaken, let us show gratitude, by which we may offer to God an acceptable service with reverence and awe."[32]

I hope that you will find a renewal in your relationship with Christ and that your awe commands you to act upon it. I hope the next time you are in church, that your awe of God affects your worship, those around you, and your walk with Christ. May you stand in amazement, kneel in respect, be still and listen. May you find the most amazing discovery of all: an Almighty God that deserves the awe and worship of all creation.

laura b. and compassion
for the Lost

Two friends of mine, Albert and Daniel, felt God leading them to host a Bible study in their apartment. God used that Bible study to be an amazing time of worship, bonding, and learning. To date, I still revere that study as one of the most amazing times in my walk with Christ. Each week, one of the members would deliver the Bible study, and we would spend time in prayer and worship.

Prayer time was especially meaningful as every person present would humble themselves in prayer to cry out to God for answers, help, and direction. One week, a young lady named Laura started to speak up to give a prayer request; however, she was so heartbroken over her request that another person had to tell us her request. Watching the tears roll down Laura's face made me think that a parent had passed away, she had been fired from her job, or had some other traumatic event happen that had adversely affected her.

On the contrary, her request was not about Laura or her life at all. Her request was this: her roommate was not a believer and she desperately wished that her roommate would come to know Christ as her Savior. Laura cried for the lost.

Her tears hit me hard because I could not remember a single time that I cried for the lost. Not some emotional, weepy, whiny, caught-up-in-the-moment tears that any emotionally hopped-up person can produce—but real tears. Through her tears, you could hear her heart straining not to break for her roommate. And there I was in the back, not able to relate at all to her desire for the lost to become followers of Christ. In that room, the contrast between the broken and the unbroken highlighted the coldness of heart that I had harbored for so long. Sure I could study the Bible, sure I could play praise choruses and get all worked up, but not once had I wept for the lost.

That night, I went back and started thinking about the words "weep" and "cold." My friend wept for the lost and I felt so cold. I started digging through the Scriptures and more times than not, I found a glimpse of Jesus' reaction towards the lost in Laura's reaction that night.

When Jesus was tired and just wanted to be alone, he didn't shun those around Him. The gospels all recount moments where Jesus saw the crowds and had compassion on them. Not pretty, dressed-up-in-a-tie-to-go-to-Sunday-School crowds, but nasty, smelly, worn out, hungry, diseased, greedy crowds, and Jesus had compassion on them. Not "I'll do better after this handout" or "I promise I'll become a missionary after you heal my son," but ungrateful, needy people who would rarely thank Jesus. And Jesus knew that they would be that way, but he still had compassion on them. And he healed them. And he fed them. And he taught them. And he loved them. And he died for them. Even as Jesus was coming into Jerusalem, in what would be the crescendo of his life leading up to his imminent death on the cross, he wept for the city of Jerusalem.[33] He had compassion for the lost.

I don't think God really cares whether or not you cry because some people cry more than others—crying is not the point. Compassion is. To see the lost—to see people outside of God's fellowship and have your heart hurt because you *want* to help them, because you *need* to help them; that is what God desires. The scriptures state that God wants "compassion, not sacrifice."[34] That scripture is very significant because there is a whole lot in the Bible about sacrifice. But God also knows that anyone can make a sacrifice—just put the money down—but not everyone can have compassion. I hope that you can find within you a heart that feels compassion—the same compassion Jesus felt when the blind men came up to him begging for their sight.[35] And know that compassion is not something we can simply conjure up within us. Pray for a heart of flesh—a heart that sees and feels what God's heart does.

In the book of Ezekiel, God spoke to the people of Israel and said, "Then I will sprinkle clean water on you, and you will be clean; I will cleanse you from all your filthiness and from all your idols. Moreover, I will give you a new heart and put a new spirit within you; and I will remove the heart of stone from your flesh and give you a heart of flesh. I will put My Spirit within you and cause you to walk in My statutes, and you will be careful to observe My ordinances."[36] God can give us a heart to see the lost and react to them with the same compassion as the heart of God. May you pray for and find compassion for those around you to help better glorify the name of God.

barely
Asian

If you ever find yourself about to die and rush into an emergency room, you probably will be asked questions that you feel are not that pertinent to the emergency—race, age, religious affiliation, mailing address, hobbies, favorite TV shows, etc. I am sure that there is a rhyme and reason to the barrage of questions, but sometimes patients wish attention would be given to the affliction and not toward seemingly superficial things. I have been to many emergency rooms as a patient due to my rambunctious nature and also have been to many others as a visitor due to the fact that my father, brother, and sister-in-law are all doctors. And of all of those emergency room visits, I haven't found one time where I liked getting asked those questions. It is probably for those reasons that when I looked for a part-time job at a hospital, I was placed in the position of Emergency Department secretary. Yes, I was the one that got to ask the questions I so greatly disliked. God has a sense of humor, doesn't he?

I had recently worked as an intern for the Baptist Student Union at Mississippi College and now had moved on to working for an emergency room, putting my history major to good use. As I went through orientation after orientation, I found myself jotting down notes, hoping and praying that I would learn to be more efficient at my job than others who I had personally suffered from.

On my first day on the job, I found myself surrounded by my supervisor and two other Emergency Department secretaries. The two other secretaries actually did the work while I observed, and my supervisor instructed me through different computer input screens.

Asking our questions was not always an easy job due to the specialties of our hospital: heart problems and psychiatric disorders. As a general rule, if someone came in our Emergency Department, they were either mentally disturbed or having a heart attack. Either way, asking a patient about his home address and race was never received with a warm welcome.

During my first day, an ambulance pulled up, and the EMTs soon wheeled an Asian-looking lady straight to room eight—our worst-case room. I watched in excitement as everyone burst into motion like ants boiling out of an ant bed after a lawn mower clipped off the top of their home. Watching it all made me a little nervous as the reality of my job started to sink in. My thoughts were interrupted by one of the workers next to me.

"What do you think she is? I think she is from the Philippines." I tried not to turn around and look at her. It struck me as really odd that the first Asian country someone would think of was the Philippines. I was about to recommend an East Asian country when my supervisor spoke up.

"You know that people who look like that can come from three different countries?" she informed all of us. "Yeah, Philippines, China, and Asia." At that point I decided I could not contribute to the conversation. I didn't want to tell my boss that Asia was a continent, and there were certainly more than three Asian countries. It being my first day of training, I felt a little too expendable to confront my boss about her geographic knowledge. As everyone nodded in agreement, I bit my lip and stared intently at the screen in front of me. While everyone seemed to be looking at the lady, trying to figure out which one of the three she was, one of the workers piped up.

"If you let me take a smoke break, I'll go ask her."

"Sure," my supervisor agreed. At that, one of our workers

walked over with cigarette pack and lighter in hand, to ask a dying lady what was her racial classification.

"She is Chinese," the worker screamed across the ER as she turned and walked towards the automatic doors. I was somewhat relieved because she gave an answer that was one of the three. I tried not to imagine what would have happened if she said she was from Japan or Myanmar. My supervisor then reached over to grab the keyboard and showed me how to input the information from the EMT sheet and our newly discovered fact that the lady was Chinese. As we cycled through the countless screens, we came to the race page.

"Uh oh," my supervisor muttered.

"What's the matter?" I asked.

"Look here." She pointed to the screen of all the choices. As expected, the screen did not list every country, but only classifications such as Caucasian, Latin American, American Indian, etc. Most importantly, Asian was listed and she coasted the mouse cursor over it and paused for a moment.

"Well, it doesn't have Chinese. We will just list her as Asian, but if she finds out, she ain't going to be happy." At that, my boss reluctantly clicked the empty box next to *Asian* to leave a bold-face check mark and solemnly went on to the insurance pages. I didn't really remember all of what she said next because I was trying my hardest not to look bewildered from the incredulous statement that a Chinese lady would be insulted at being called an Asian. Also, I was making a mental note of whom I would call after work to tell about what happened and admonish them to study their world geography. I did learn one thing that day, though. At our hospital, the Chinese are Asians… barely.

Like this experience in the emergency room, sometimes we do the right things or come up with the right answers, but the reasons or methods are a little off. Or a lot off. Take doing good deeds for example. If I give someone a ride because a person needs a ride, he gets to wherever he needed to go. That is simple. Well, kindness happened, but why did it happen? Did I give the ride because I wanted something in return? Did I give the person the ride just because it was the right thing to do and I was brought up in a polite family? Or did I give him the ride in an effort to serve because, as a believer, I need to emulate the greatest servant of all.

Why does it matter? Being good is, in fact, good, and that is the point, isn't it? Well, it does matter, and the reason is this—who does it point to? If I do something nice, because I am a nice person, people will walk away thinking, "What a nice guy..." If I am nice because my father taught me to be nice, people will walk away thinking, "That guy's father sure must have been a nice guy..." The same idea applies if I help someone because I am a Christian and I love them through Christ. They will walk away thinking, "What that guy says he believes must be important for him to treat me so nice..."

To change the "why" in what we do is difficult. My parents brought me up in a home that helped others. I always did good things because I was part of my family and what I did reflected on my parents. I can recall the countless speeches from mom and dad that began with, "When you leave here, your actions will reflect on us..." As a result of my upbringing, I did nice things mainly because my parents would approve. However, during my junior year in college, I started taking the *Experiencing God* Bible study and was serving through the Baptist Student Union on campus. Through interactions with others, talking with the director, Keith Cating, and through what I learned in my Bible study, I found out that I was actually proud of my "humility" and I was doing the "right thing" for me and others and not really for God. This realization came with a "so what?" response. If I am doing what is right, who cares *why* I am doing it?

I am rather prideful at times and hate to be wrong, so I questioned this new mode of living that took my past performance into question. In addition to that, I was the only one who really knew about my out-of-whack reasoning—no one else really could see my motives. If they couldn't see my motives, I really shouldn't have to make a change. That sounded reasonable, so I didn't change immediately.

Despite my arguments against changing what I was doing, I still felt deep down that perhaps my motives did matter. I finally decided to put this "motives" rationale to test the day my *Experiencing God* Bible study rolled back around. It was one of those rainy winter days that was yucky. As I grabbed my Bible Study book and flipped through it to see how many lessons I was too lazy to complete, I told God that I would like to do something for his sake and not anyone else's. I said if he wanted it to be that way, I would be glad if I could give someone a ride who was walking in the rain. This was definitely a God-sized task because not many people walk in the rain. In addition, Mississippi was the reigning champion of being the most overweight state in the Union, so not too many of us walk in general.

I jumped in my truck and headed towards campus. I thought if anyone was going to be walking in the rain, I would find him on the university's campus. I turned across from the mall into the Jackson Avenue entrance and I cruised through campus looking for a suspect to offer a ride to. I made it all the way through campus and onto University Avenue without seeing anyone. I am sure I was thinking, "So much for that" or something along those lines as I pulled up to the four-way stop in front of the BSU. There I noticed a man walking in the rain with his collar pulled up and his head hunched down to keep out of the rain. I initially thought that he wasn't going where I was going—I needed to take a left and he looked as if he were heading straight towards the Square—but I chided myself for the thought and rolled down my window. I asked him if he needed a ride, and he gladly accepted and hopped into my truck. Before I could ask him where he wanted to go, he turned to me and said, "God must have sent you 'cause I was just praying for a ride." My only response was "Yes, yes, he did." We introduced ourselves and chatted on the way to James Food Center, and I knew that there was a *why* to what I was doing and a *why* to what had happened. After dropping him off, I turned back towards the BSU.

I was late for my Bible study, but I learned more in that moment than I would have if I had been on time. It was in that moment that I knew why there needed to be a "why" in what we do. We need to continually point towards God.

In the Bible, countless people were selfless and sought to maintain the "why" in what they did by constantly giving all credit to God. The Old Testament prophets always gave credit to God and only spoke his words. Two New Testament examples are well known—John the Baptist and Jesus.

Who would work and work to develop a following and the moment Jesus walks up they step down and let all of their followers leave to follow Jesus? John the Baptist gave up his life's work. His lasting accomplishments—to prepare the way and to teach disciples—were given away as soon as Jesus arrived on the scene. How could he do such a thing? He established *why* he was preaching and teaching before he began. I am sure the people praised John for his teachings and his radical devotion. And what was his response? "I am preparing the way for another who is so great that I am unworthy to touch his dirty sandals." He definitely was not keeping glory for himself.

And Jesus? What did he do? He was God's son, and he repeatedly proclaimed that he could only do what he did through his Father in Heaven. Jesus could have had the whole world eating out of his hand—he performed miracle after miracle, and a lot of the people wanted him to be their king. He could have had it all—and that is exactly what Satan offered him, but to no avail. Jesus already had the "why" set in stone before he set out in his ministry—his Father's will. For his Father's glory. Even when it hurts. Even when it seemed like he would lose friends, followers, and faith—to God be the glory.

I hope that we can take the good that we do and make sure that our actions point to God and to nothing else. Because God alone is worthy of glory and praise.

getting lost in
the Woods

Another time I was lost in the woods was when I was in the Webe-los. I was pretty new to the whole scouting thing, but I enjoyed my affiliation with this "paramilitary group" nonetheless. The main thing I liked about scouting was the patches; in fact, my involvement in scouts primarily stemmed from my fascination with patches. I love patches! Growing up my mom had her banner of badges from her days as a Girl Scout, and I hoped to outdo her with my experiences as a scout.

My most memorable attempt of trying to earn a patch was when our troop set out to earn the orienteering badge. Our guides were a mechanic and a banker and "we" were fifteen elementary school kids. It probably appeared more like two men trying to herd kittens, but our leaders were patient and tried their best to teach us the basics.

Our lesson on the "basics" was given to us in the church parking lot. Our leaders put up orange cones, and we stood in the middle and called out what compass heading corresponded to each cone. Then they reconfigured the exercise by placing more cones and calling out a compass heading. We had to point to which cone was called out. Practicing was fun and wasn't tricky; all we did was stand still and call out numbers. Most of us mused that orienteering wasn't that difficult because it had a lot of similarities with a game of bingo or Battleship.

A week later, we got together and learned about true north and magnetic north—I am not really sure what the differences are exactly, but I learned that if a hiker uses the wrong one, he will get lost. Along with our true north vs. magnetic north lecture, we set a date when we would brave the woods by navigating through the nearby 7,200 acre hunting reserve. We were excited about the trip. Our leaders told us to wear hiking shoes and that all that we would need to bring was insect repellant and a compass.

After our meeting, I immediately went home and packed enough for a small expedition to the moon. I had an old external frame backpack that I had bought from Service Merchandise with my allowance and I packed it to the hilt. I included binoculars, peanut butter crackers, two randomly selected books, my swim goggles and snorkel, duct tape, a wood saw, machete, survival knife, jacket, and two packages of kippered herring. I then placed my expedition pack in the foyer of our house and anxiously awaited the day of the hike.

The day of the hike finally rolled around and my father dropped me off at the church where the scouts were loaded into the back of two pick-ups. I am sure loading fifteen kids into the beds of two pick-ups was not part of the safety badge, but that was for a later week and we piled in. En route to the game reserve, we passed a field that had over twenty wild turkeys, and the trucks screeched to a halt, so our leaders could view the wonderful sight. They saw it as wonderful not because the natural view was aesthetically pleasing, but because turkey season was to open in a few days and the birds were future targets.

Upon our arrival, we all piled out at the entrance of the game reserve and divided up into two groups. Then the leaders rethought their plan, and we all converged into one large group and headed out. Our goal was to hike out into the woods for one mile, choose another bearing, hike for another mile, and then turn again and head back to our point of origin. That plan seemed easy enough, so we headed out, each of us with a compass on a lanyard outstretched in front of us as we forged into the wilderness. In addition to my compass, I had my enormous backpack. At the beginning of the hike, most of the other scouts scoffed at me as I lugged around my supplies for a family of eight, but I enjoyed having gizmos, so I shrugged off their snide remarks.

We had hiked for almost an hour when we all came to a halt. One of our leaders, the banker, stopped because he discovered some markings on the ground that indicated there were more turkeys in the area. He gathered us around and showed us how he could use the lead-tipped bullets in his .357 to make marks on the map. Little did we know that "being prepared" didn't mean to bring a pencil, but multi-purpose, high-velocity bullets instead.

While our leader marked the map, we took a break. Several scouts walked over to the bank of a creek to the right of the turkey scratches and started playing in the water. Others climbed a funny looking tree that had a crooked trunk while the rest of us just plopped down on the forest floor and drank water. After our short break, we set off again towards our destination. Within another hour, however, we all came to a halt again. Our leader found more turkey scratches, and he had the same demonstration—pull out map, pull out revolver, pull out bullet, mark map, put all things where they belong—and we were off again. And then there were more turkey scratches. And then *more* turkey scratches. I was starting to think we were in a turkey village and that our leader shouldn't make threatening moves because those ugly birds certainly outnumbered us two to one.

As our leader kneeled down to start his bullet-etching routine, he glanced at the scouts playing in the ditch and the others climbing on the funny-looking tree. He then pulled out the map, but didn't continue with his routine. He looked around, looked at his compass, and then looked at his watch. Those of us who had plopped down on the grass started giggling as we watched our leader turn the map to and fro. He frantically tried to figure out which way was up and how we got where we were—and more importantly, why we kept coming back to the same spot. The second leader, the mechanic, approached the banker and they talked in hushed tones, glancing around at us, at the tree line and then back at the map. Next, they called us all together for an impromptu meeting. They told us that we were "a little lost," but most likely we were in one of two places on the map. I figure they said we were a little lost because we were lost in a place we had been at least three times before. Because of our "lost-ness," they were going to split us up into two groups—one leader for each group—and we would set off in different directions. Among the scouts present, we nicknamed the two groups by our leaders' occupations, and unfortunately I landed in the "banker" group.

He told us that we would head due east and the other group was going to head north. Whichever group made it to a road or house first, they would call for help—not because we needed help, but because that is what people do in these situations. The other group would just continue until they found a road or house, too. All of us knew that we were going to be the group that hiked the longest because our group leader was the one that got us lost in the first place.

As we started hiking, the grumbling picked up. Our leader must have known that we were talking about him behind his back because he picked up his pace to a near run. I guess he figured that if we were out of breath from hiking *so* fast, we couldn't badmouth him. As everyone hiked on with a sour looking expression, I was grinning because I still had all of my food in my bag. The people that made fun of me were going to be real sorry now that we were lost in the middle of nowhere. *Too bad for them,* I thought, as I smirked at everyone. I thought it was going to be quite adventurous to spend the night in the woods, too, but our leader didn't share the same sentiment.

It was now 2:30 in the afternoon, and our leader was starting to look a little edgy. For the next three hours, we hiked and hiked in a straight line, and our leader very careful to keep his compass bearing dead on. In fact, we would not even veer from our direction to go through briars or privet hedge—we would just plow through headfirst, "ouching" and "ewwing" the whole way.

Finally, our little group came upon a cabin in the woods—a hunting camp—and our leader recognized the cabin. He promptly found a way into the cabin, located a phone, and called anyone and everyone to see if the other group had made it out. In hindsight, maybe he just told us he knew who lived there, so we wouldn't think twice about it when he broke into the cabin. Two hours later, at dusk, the rest of our group arrived, and all of them looked rather shaken by the event. By nightfall, a truck came and we all piled in to be taken to where we left the other vehicles. After swapping vehicles, we began the long drive home, all of us quiet from exhaustion and hunger from our long hike in the woods.

On the way home and in subsequent scout meetings, no one expressed a desire to get the patch for orienteering. We didn't talk about it for two reasons—first, our leader didn't want to bring it up because he knew it was his fault, and second, we found out that our leader really didn't think it was humorous when little fifth graders bring up how a turkey's sense of direction is better than a banker's.

In theory, our route was simple. Go to point A, then to point B and then to point C. In reality, that is not the easiest thing to do. In walking with a compass, a few degrees off can multiply to be a lot off when the hiker arrives at the finishing point. To complicate the difficulty, our leader took his eyes off of his end goal—we went from earning an orienteering patch to a "turkey hunter" patch that didn't exist.

As for the trip, I did learn a lot—we learned what turkey scratches looked like, that we could use bullets as pencils (but I would have to wait for eight years before we could purchase those ballistic number twos), and that a snorkel and goggles are not needed on a hike in the woods. The only problem is that what I learned was not the purpose of the trip and, therefore, the trip was a failure.

How many times have we set out to do something and then found ourselves distracted? As for me, *daily* would be the answer to that question. Distractions, lack of self-discipline, and the desire to be entertained all compete for my attention in my journey. While we are here on Earth, what exactly is our goal? On the hike, we all wanted a patch—less than two square inches—as an accolade for our accomplishments. Distractions along the way prevented us from reaching our goal. In life, do we get distracted and lose what God's wants us to strive for? Paul knew what his end goal was, and he also knew that other things were competing for his allegiance. In the book of Hebrews, the author says that we need to put aside everything that entangles us so we can better run the race.[37] Paul wrote the Corinthians that in running the race, that only one wins a prize.[38] Therefore, Christians should run their "race" of life as if there were only one winner. This theme is a continuous thread through Paul's writings. Later in a letter to Timothy, he wrote that if anyone competes as an athlete, "he does not win the prize unless he competes according to the rules."[39]

If Christians are supposed to have an end goal, strive towards it as if in a race, and also adhere to the rules, what exactly is the end goal and what are the rules? Theologians have written volumes on these two questions, and the Sadducees and the Pharisees thought they had a good grasp on the answers as well. Regardless of the complexities of many purported answers to these questions, Jesus' answer is simple. One can see His simple approach in his teachings of the New Testament, especially in his dialogue with the religious leaders of the day.

One day, while the Pharisees and Sadducees were trying to test Jesus's knowledge of his father, they asked him what the "great commandment of the law" was. Jesus's reply was this: "'You shall love the Lord with all your heart, and with all your soul, and with all your mind.' This is the great and foremost commandment. The second is like it, 'You shall love your neighbor as yourself.' On these two commandments depend the whole Law and the Prophets."[40] Where many would claim that was a great oversimplification of the Old Testament, Jesus was quite sure of what he was saying—do these two things and you will fulfill all of the Law and the Prophets. Amazing. Also one will find in the books of Luke and John two key verses: John 14:4: "I am the way, the truth and the life. No man comes unto the father except by me" and Luke 9:23: "If anyone wishes to come after Me, he must deny himself, and take up his cross daily and follow Me."

Some may find the rules in these verses rather rigid and unfair. What happens if I want to look for turkey scratches? What happens if I want look for other things and not look for what I am "supposed" to seek? That just isn't fair. In the beginning, that is the way I saw my parents' rules and the Bible, too. During childhood everything seems unfair because the rules require us to take ourselves out of first place. Now that I am older and wiser—wiser meaning I have fallen many times and gotten lost many times while pursuing other things—I find these simple rules rather freeing. How simple can it possibly get? Rather than trying to convolute things so there is a hierarchy where we can *ooh* and *ahh* at each other's achievements, Jesus seeks simple devotion that puts God first. And in keeping God first, we find ourselves helping those around us in order to give more glory and honor to God.

Not only are the rules simple, the goal is wonderful. Echoes of this goal are heard in the Psalms and are seen through scripture from the beginning when God walked in the garden to the cross where God sent the ultimate sacrifice to renew the relationship. "I would have despaired unless I had believed that I would see the goodness of the Lord in the land of the living."[41] To know God. To see Him and worship Him.

Why does Christ state that people must deny themselves daily, take up their cross, and follow him? It isn't because he is unjust. It is because he knows that to know him is the best thing that can possibly happen. Because knowing him leads to fellowship with an Almighty God who has plans for us, sings over us with praise, paid the ultimate sacrifice for us, and is preparing a place for us. He wants us to win the race. He wants to give us pure love, indestructible hope, true kindness and great courage. How wonderful those gifts would be, and they truly can be ours because they are promised to us in scripture. And, yet, there are some people who trade all of that away for the occasional turkey scratch while lost in the woods.

Dear God,

Thank you for being a God who has plans for me. Thank you for loving me, singing over me with praise, for being my comfort, and for giving me a hope and a future. Please help me keep focused on You—may I throw away all that impedes me and may I run the race set before me with vigor and devotion. Thank you.

Amen.

731

The numbers 731 don't hold any special significance for most people; probably around 5/6 of the world would think it is a telephone prefix or the number of a favorite team. These numbers, however, do mean something to the Chinese. 731 is the name of a medical experiment station that the Japanese built in Heilongjiang province in the Pingfang district. The Japanese failed to destroy this medical experiment station as the curtains were closing on World War II. Now 731 is a museum of Japanese war atrocities which have been declared war crimes by the United Nations.

For those of you who don't remember much of history class, the Japanese invaded China, Korea, Singapore, Papua New Guinea, Indonesia… well, pretty much every corner of East Asia and Southeast Asia. The Japanese conquerors were not known for being very nice to the people they conquered, for the invading Japanese forces followed a creed that they were superior to those they conquered. The prisoners who were captured and kept in 731 were referred to as "logs" or "monkeys" to denote that they were no longer human. In China, the Japanese army massacred countless people—and thousands of these died during medical experiments—hence, 731.

The Japanese did very unorthodox things to their prisoners just out of a sick medical fascination, which during that time they thought was fine and dandy. The Japanese continued to do experiments on the Chinese and other POWs at 731 and many other labs until the tide of the war turned; soon Mao ZeDong and his troops, along with Allied air support, started the long and hard push to force the Japanese out of China and back to Japan. As Japan saw defeat, they realized that doing terrible things to people when they were winning seemed alright, but if they lost the war, they didn't want their enemies to remember how bad they were. They quickly went about trying to destroy, bury, and burn any evidence that existed of their atrocities, but many of their well-made structures survived their inflicted self-destructions. As a result 731 remained intact. Not only was it physically intact, but it contained within it heaps of evidence, photographs, and data taken during the experiments. That is similar to finding a mass murderer's home and then finding his diary—but on a much, much larger scale. And today, one can visit 731 to relive the horror or surf the web and find countless websites dedicated to the tragedy.

So what is the big deal about it? Sure it was bad, but lots of other bad things happened during the war. The Japanese formally surrendered on September 2, 1945—and that is a long time ago. The only people who directly suffered from Japan's atrocities have all reached or passed septuagenarian status, so why would they remember it? The Chinese government took offense to the deeds (of course, who wouldn't?), but today the roots of their dislike for what the Japanese did and for the Japanese themselves is this—they didn't confess to their deeds and they did not apologize. Not only did they not confess, but many of the perpetrators of the crimes went on to have prominent careers within Japan and some of the doctors went on to give medical lectures based on research conducted at 731. And today, 731 stands among many other testaments to mankind's atrocities. As a result of the lack of confession on the part of the Japanese and the lack of forgiveness of the Chinese, relationships have been strained between the two countries and remain that way for crimes committed seventy years prior.

This breach in a relationship between China and Japan was a terrible, terrible thing. Today, these neighbors could profit from each other and could help each other, but they find themselves delicately operating in a fragile friendship hurting from wounds that will not heal. This lack of healing between the two countries continues with no obvious end in sight and it serves as an example of what happens between individuals on a daily basis.

To emulate these two countries by breaking a relationship is quite simple; here is a step-by-step guide on how many relationships end:

Step #1 Person A offends Person B. Person B can be a friend, stranger, or relative.

Step #2 Person B is offended and wants an apology, but he usually does not verbalize the need for an apology because an apology is "expected."

Step #3 Person A does not offer an apology. He may or may not know that Person B was offended.

Step #4 Person B now needs an apology, but an apology will no longer suffice. Out of principle (pride) Person B ceases communicating with Person A

Step #5 Person A quits talking to Person B because of Person B's odd behavior.

There you have it—five simple steps, and any relationship can be ruined. How often do we find ourselves in a position like Person A or Person B? Pretty soon Person A and Person B spend all of their time maintaining the memory of how the relationship was broken rather than working on fixing it. Although we do not build physical monuments to how our relationships break, we find ourselves erecting emotional monuments nonetheless: "Oh, I haven't been to that restaurant since so-and-so starting treating me so strange" or "I really don't like to go to that Sunday school class because so-and-so is there and I don't think…"

Although Person A was the one who caused the offense, it is up to both of them to bring the relationship back to a point where it will work again. As part of human nature, we don't like to be hurt and we really don't like to forgive those who "don't deserve forgiveness." "Why should I forgive them? They did it and they aren't even sorry for it." Asking questions like these is a surefire method of keeping the relationship broken.

How can a relationship that is broken be restored? The best way to mend relationships is to take Christ's advice—forgive. Forgive those who transgress against us, forgive our enemies, forgive one another. Forgive. And Christ, the perfect example, even forgave people as he was bleeding on the cross. Now that is amazing. Most of us can find it in ourselves to forgive someone a year or two later—add more years if they didn't apologize—but Christ forgave—and still forgives—in the moment of offense. Christ wants us to give forgiveness rather than building monuments that impede our relationships. And Christ forgave to show us how.

Jesus could have had numerous monuments: "Oh, here is the temple where the people don't really get what I am saying." "Here is the boat where Peter really couldn't hack it while walking on water." "Here is the kitchen where Martha focused more on what she was cooking than on me." But Christ didn't waste time harboring grudges. He freely forgave and moved forward with the relationships.

Forgiveness definitely was a frequent topic in Jesus' teaching. It is a hard topic not to address in a land that was under foreign occupation. No doubt the unjustness of the Roman rule weighed heavily on all of the people. Jesus addressed the requirements of Roman rule when he taught that people should walk two miles instead of one. To walk one mile was a requirement—a Roman soldier could force people to help carry things because they were under Roman rule, so they had to for one mile. While I probably would have reached the mile and left thinking, *No good, Roman punk officer. Jerk. Can't wait till they all go away...* Jesus taught to go another mile just to show what love is and who God is. Forgiveness in the moment allows love to overpower the offense—for both the offender and the offended.

Once, Peter asked Jesus "how often shall my brother sin against me and I forgive him?"[42] Peter's guess of seven times fell short to Jesus' answer of seventy times seven. When I read this text, I have always imagined one of the disciples getting on Peter's nerves, probably arguing about where they were going to sit in Heaven or something like that. As Peter turned and told the other disciples that they better leave him alone or else, they smugly replied that he shouldn't hit a disciple because Jesus taught to forgive. This being the eighth time, Peter turned to Jesus and asked his question hoping to get permission to slug the perpetrator. With fists clenched and jaw set, Peter listened in dissatisfaction to the answer that he must wait four hundred and eighty-two more times before he could start swinging.

Why so many times? Jesus verbalizes his reason for forgiveness in the Sermon on the Mount. "For if you forgive others for their transgressions, your heavenly Father will also forgive you. But if you do not forgive others, then your Father will not forgive your transgressions."[43] Can you think of a better reason to forgive? Another reason, I believe, is to help us understand who God is. If we forgive someone, we understand one who forgives. Also, forgiveness forces *us* to change—it softens a heart hardened by grudges and causes us to yield to those around us. As we struggle to forgive endlessly, we start to understand who God is. Who could possibly forgive more than a perfect, holy God? Who really doesn't *have* to forgive? God forgives because he chooses to forgive us, to love us, and to reinstate us into a loving relationship with himself—a mighty, awesome God. And He wants us to take that forgiveness and give it to others so that they too may find themselves in a loving relationship with a mighty, awesome God.

Pray, then, in this way:

"Our Father who is in heaven, hallowed be Your name. Your kingdom come. Your will be done, on earth as it is in heaven. Give us this day our daily bread. And forgive us our debts, as we also have forgiven our debtors. And do not lead us into temptation, but deliver us from evil. For Yours is the kingdom and the power and the glory forever. Amen."[44]

gas stations
and Lunch

Oxford, Mississippi is a lovely town. It is home to the University of Mississippi and William Faulkner's Roanoke. It is a land steeped in tradition, a great love for football, and always is bustling with social events. Oxford's crowning jewel is the Square. It has many delightful stores, unique restaurants, and bakeries that entice college students to spend up to their last dime on food and entertainment. When I was in school, I did my best to eat out as long as there was a positive balance in my checking account and probably could have bought a portion of a Caribbean island for what I paid for eating out.

One of my favorite places to eat in Oxford was located just off the Square and I ate there probably twice a week. The name of my favorite restaurant? McPhail's Chevron at Four Corners. Yes, it happened to be a gas station located across from Abner's Chicken and Bancorpsouth. If a patron would like, he or she could eat breakfast, lunch, and supper at the gas station. This isn't fast food fare either—green beans, biscuits (the sausage and cheese is quite nice), chicken-on-a-stick (best at two in the morning), fried catfish, chicken, macaroni and cheese—you name it, this place has it. If I could've afforded it, I would have gone everyday for lunch my junior year in college—it was only $4.99 for two vegetables, one meat, cornbread or a biscuit, and sweet tea. Not only was it cheap, it was probably the healthiest meal that I would eat all day. Since I lived off campus, I would usually swing by the Chevron, grab two canned Cokes and a plate lunch, and then go to the BSU, where I would enjoy my fine cuisine and kill an hour—or four—while chatting with whoever dropped by.

One day, I swung by the BSU with my two cans of coke and a plate lunch of green beans, hamburger steak with gravy on rice, fried okra, and a piece of cornbread. As I made my way to my usual seat, I poked my head into the associate director's office to say "hey." Ms. Beverly inquired about the lunch I had been bringing with me and I told her that I bought it at Chevron. The gas station is the closest place to get food from the BSU, unless you duck into someone's apartment, so I was surprised at her reaction. She was incredulous that I would eat at a gas station and even more that a gas station would have plate lunches. Sure, most gas stations have those stale sandwiches wrapped in plastic that one can microwave, but as for being able to purchase a plate lunch—that was shocking to her. I was taken aback as well—I figured if something was common in Mississippi, other states in the South would have something similar. And since Ms. Beverly was from Texas, and everything is bigger in Texas, I just figured every gas station would have had a buffet or a sit-down restaurant. She informed me that getting lunch at a gas station isn't normal or at least should not be normal, but after trying some of the cornbread, she said it was delicious and it tasted like cornbread from home.

Not only did I find it amazing that she didn't eat lunch in gas stations in her home state, but I also found it amazing that she never realized that she could eat lunch at almost any gas station in town. Obie's Chevron, Lindsay's Chevron, McPhail's Chevron, the Shell station on South Lamar, James Food Center (which has a grocery store, gas station, deli, and post office), and the Chevron gas station across from CB Webb all had great lunches that tasted great and were inexpensive. These monuments to the Blue Light Laws of yesteryear made it where a person couldn't drive anywhere through town without going past a gas station with barbeque, plate lunches or turkey legs, and yet Ms. Beverly had missed it. Despite the fact that I ate many times in her presence and there were stores offering plate lunches all around her, she didn't notice. This is not any deficiency on her part—she didn't know to look in filling stations for fried foods. In fact, no one ever told her. How was she supposed to know if no one ever told her? She didn't know because I had eaten in her presence many times and never told her. Well, that was my fault. And what was my excuse? I don't feel comfortable telling others about where I like to eat. I just like to live by example by eating there on a twice a week basis and maybe they will notice the difference in my food when I am around. Of course, I don't say that nor do I think it, but that sounds too familiar, doesn't it?

This is the excuse used by too many Christians—myself included. We live our lives with a hope and a love that others lack, but we live it in a self-imposed secrecy. We work with unbelievers, we eat out with unbelievers, we hang out with unbelievers, and we don't tell them about what we believe. When they are still unbelieving, we think, "Well, I just live by example. They should see the difference in me. It is up to them to ask. I mean, there is a church on every corner of this town." If Jesus thought that silence was the best method in communicating the gospel to the world, publishers would not be able to make a "red letter" version of the Bible. Jesus didn't only live out a Godly life, he verbalized it; he told everyone about his father in Heaven even when he knew that they would reject him for it.

In Romans, Paul asks "How will they believe in Him whom they have not heard? And how will they hear without a preacher?"[45] When a person is getting a haircut, while he is checking out at the local grocery store, or chatting with a neighbor about the day's happenings—he may just be the "preacher" who needs to talk about Jesus. Is it uncomfortable? It can be. Is being uncomfortable a reason not to tell? Never is and never will be. Is it hard to believe that people can not know about Jesus even when there are three preachers on television at any given moment, and there are billboards in town about various churches? It can be. But is it possible for a person to want to know the answer, to have the answer right in front of him, and somehow not get the answer? It happens all the time. I do it when I am supposed to assemble something or get lost while driving. Countless people have experienced this while sitting in an Algebra class. So don't be surprised that a lost person could want to know the answer, have the answer right in front of him, and yet not be able to understand the answer.

This world needs to hear about Christ and they need to be told that he is the answer, the hope, and the peace that they have been missing. When they are told, they are brought into fellowship with us, the church, and with God. In 1 John, John writes that the believers told about what they had heard and seen, so the ones who heard would be taken into fellowship.[46]

We need to tell the lost world about the salvation we have through Christ Jesus. We need to tell them, so they can worship God and find hope and peace. Not only do we need to tell them so they can know God, but we also need to tell them to help us gain a greater understanding of who God is. It is said that the best way to learn something is to teach it—this same principle applies when I tell others about what I believe. Paul wrote that as we share with others about our faith, we come to a greater understanding of every good thing we have in Jesus Christ.[47] As we tell others, we share hope and we also learn more about the hope we have. How wonderful is that?

I hope that as you go throughout your day at work or at play, you discover ways to tell others about what you believe. Not only living out your faith, but verbalizing it in a way that helps others understand and see Jesus, perhaps for the first time. It is one thing to miss out on a plate lunch from a filling station, but it is another thing to miss out on an eternity with your creator. May you be the one to break the silence and tell those around you why you live the way you do.

Dear God,

Thank you for the hope that you offer us. Thank you for showing us the way—not only through Christ's life on earth, but through his words. May we have the courage to love others, tell others, and lead others in efforts to let them know you. In all things, may your creation know you and worship you for who you are. Thank you. Amen.

how a chinese bible finds
a Chinese Boy

I have a confession to make: I like math. Now before anyone chooses to write me off as a nutcase, nerd or geek, understand that I did not say "I like math class." To me that is different.

Math helps me put things in perspective. For example, I will do math to help explain something—like driving to a destination or saving money for a toy or whatever. Math helps me out.

Something I started doing as of late is applying math to Bible stories. For instance, I have heard the story of Gideon and his army so many times that I can close my eyes and see the troops gathered by the stream, slurping water out of their hands, or blowing trumpets on a hilltop. I have heard it so many times that the story actually has lost some of its miraculousness. Yeah, Gideon laid out a fleece. Wet fleece, dry ground. Vice versa. He had a bunch of people in an army. Then he had very few people. Blow the trumpets, yada yada yada, and the other army kills themselves blah, blah.

While sitting in church, I started to try to make it real again, so I jotted in the margins the number of people before and after God narrowed the size of the army. Gideon started out with 32,000 people and after the ones who were scared or drank water like animals left, Gideon only had 300 people. That is a big difference. To represent the difference, I tried to imagine what it would be like to have two armies, one with 32,000 and one with 300, march through town in a parade. If each group marched by with rows of ten people across and they kept five feet in between each row, just how long would the parade be? The 32,000 group would have 3,200 rows and at five feet between each row, that would be a parade with a length of 16,000 feet. That would be a parade that would stretch for over fifty-three football fields. That is an impressive army. In fact, that kind of army would strike fear into the hearts of those who would see it.

Now let's take the 300. The 300 would make up thirty rows and at five feet between each row, that would be a parade of 150 feet. Or half a football field. Knowing that—and knowing that Gideon saw his army when it was at 32,000 and at 300—one can imagine that Gideon had a little trepidation going into this ordeal.

Another time math helped me put things into perspective is when God used me while working on the Mississippi Gulf Coast. I had just finished my master's degree and was so burned out from studying, I sought a job that required little to no thought at all. The result was that I ran a weed-eater at the Gulf Coast Baptist Assembly in Pass Christian. I packed up most of my belongings (they all fit in my pick-up) and moved into the dorm. I brought with me the essentials—guitar, computer, kayak paddle, and books. Among my books were two Chinese Bibles—a New Testament that I received as a gift from workers in Liaoning Province and another I bought while in Hong Kong.

The Assembly ran youth camps all summer and our job was to keep it looking nice for the campers and to make sure their visit went with ease. Fish Robinson was the speaker for the youth camps and we occasionally would run into each other and talk about how the camp was going. If the grounds crew had time, we would try to clean up in time for the nightly group assembly and worship service. One week, a youth group from Amory, Mississippi, came and brought with them a Chinese high school exchange student. Some of the other maintenance workers asked me if I had met the Chinese boy, but I hadn't.

That week, God started to convict me to give the Bible I bought in Hong Kong to the Chinese boy and to tell you the truth, I really didn't want to. In addition to being my Bible, it was a study tool for my Chinese and a souvenir from the Christmas in China program I had participated in the year before. It had an audio CD in the back that was a recording of the plan of salvation, and I had planned to study it and learn it. As the week dragged on, my clutched fingers around my possessions started to yield and finally I told God that, yes, I would give that Chinese boy my Bible, but I still didn't want to. I had the decision to make, and I begrudgingly made the decision for what God wanted and not for what I wanted.

The next to the last day of camp, I walked in around eleven o'clock at night to where the "faculty" mail boxes were. I knew which faculty member's group the Chinese boy belonged to, so I just planned on sticking the Bible in the group leader's box. As I walked in, Fish was hanging out in the lobby. As I approached him, I stated that I had a Chinese Bible for the Chinese kid with the Amory group. His face lit up and he exclaimed that he had been praying for God to provide a Chinese Bible for the boy because the Chinese boy had just accepted Christ as his Lord and Savior.

As I handed him the Bible, Fish asked if the boy would understand the Bible. I told him that since the Bible was from Hong Kong, it had traditional characters, not the simplified text, so it may be difficult to read if the boy was from Mainland China. Fish smiled again—he told me that the boy was from Hong Kong. Not only did God answer his prayer, but he answered it completely and perfectly. I left Fish with the Bible—he was amazed at God's workings on how a Chinese boy from Amory could get a Bible while in Pass Christian. I walked away glad that I let go of my small possessions, so I could be part of God's greater plan.

That night, I sat in bed thinking about it—I really wouldn't have thought much about it except for the fact that the boy was from Hong Kong. What were the chances that I would bring the Bible from Hong Kong? I had several Chinese Bibles and the only reason I brought that Bible was because I wanted to study the audio part. In fact, I almost did not bring the Bible, but only the CD. The reason I brought the Bible is that it had a CD holder for the CD and I couldn't find an extra as I packed for the trip.

I then started thinking about the probability that a Chinese boy from Hong Kong would end up in Amory, Mississippi—that must have been a drastic change. He went from a city that has almost 15,000 people per square mile to an isolated, rural community. And then what were the chances that his host family would bring him to church? That his family would foot the bill for him to go to camp? And his church would go to summer camp on the Mississippi gulf coast? Those definitely aren't good gambling odds.

Then I started thinking about my side of things. What were the chances that China would have a SARS outbreak, and I would leave China to start graduate work at the University of Southern Mississippi? And then what were the chances that I would go with USM to Hong Kong and the one souvenir I bought was that Bible? And then that I would be so burned out from school that I would be the only person with a master's degree using a weed-eater? Those are the immediate decisions that took place to allow one, newly-graduated guy with a Chinese Bible to end up in a town where a high school exchange-student from Hong Kong would be headed. The more I thought about it the more innumerable the decisions were and how what happened was for all practical purposes impossible. To think that I sometimes doubt God has a plan!

From the time I ran into a group of Chinese men in a mall in Jackson, Mississippi, events happened that had allowed me to travel to China in 1997 and from then God had been orchestrating a little event—insignificant to most—that would happen almost seven years later in a small town on the Mississippi Gulf Coast. Our God is an amazing God. He has plans, amazing plans, that give us and our sisters and brothers in Christ an amazing hope.

And all I had to do was to go along with the miracles of God. Even today I am glad that I yielded and gave up my Chinese Bible. If I had told God no—that I was keeping my Bible—I may have never known that the Chinese boy had become a Christian, that

Fish was praying for a Bible, and, most importantly, that God had a plan for me, that Chinese boy, and that book I bought a year prior.

This is just one of many, many events that has happened in my life that math helped clarify for me. The more I thought about the event, the more I realized how "God-sized" the event really was.

The same goes with any event in your life. Next time you have an opportunity to help someone, think about it. Afterwards, after you have let God use you, reflect on the many, many decisions that were made that allowed you to be at that place at that point in time. Surely you will find in the mundane or the small "accidents" in life the truly miraculous.

$500 bills for beggars—
God's Touch Revisited

Beggars are commonly seen anywhere in the world. Someone will always be asking for a few dollars for gas, so he can make it home or holding a sign that says, "Homeless. I am hungry. God bless."

Along with beggars, however, there are the ever-present rumors about beggars. I have heard that beggars have an underground organization and that they live in mansions and/or drive nice cars because they are hoodwinking the general public. The same persons that repeat these rumors are the ones who say that is the reason they do not give money to beggars.

I, however, *have* to give to beggars. My reason for wanting to give comes from my father's example.

My father once gave money to a beggar at a rest stop in Florida—the beggar was twenty-something, hadn't had a bath in a while, and was hippie-esque in appearance. After my father gave him five dollars and entered our family van, he turned to me and explained why he did what he did. He said that he had no idea if the boy was genuine and if he really needed gas money. He also would never know if he needed money because he was destitute or he had spent his last dime on alcohol or drugs. He had no way of knowing those things. Dad said he did know that the boy expressed a need and he was able to help him in that need. That part is our responsibility. If the boy took the money and pocketed it, or if he bought enough gas to make it home—well, that was the boy's responsibility. That made sense to me and still makes sense, so I have used my father's "kindness over doubt" *modus operandi* as my own.

With that as my legacy to follow, I see beggars as people in need despite the few or many who try to abuse the kindness of strangers. That does not mean I fork out cash at every intersection when I see cardboard placards, but it does mean I try to help when I can.

Once, while visiting a friend of mine in Indonesia, we traveled to Yogyakarta to visit a few historical sites. We stayed at a hotel a little distance from the shopping district and anytime we walked anywhere in the town, we were assaulted by beggars and peddlers. In front of one store in particular, there were several older ladies who sat against the storefront and begged for handouts. The first day, I felt compelled to give them some money, so I placed the money in each of their hands and walked on. I never really liked throwing money into cups or baskets because I thought that was dehumanizing like throwing a bone to a dog.

That first night, I started thinking about what I gave them. There were six ladies in all, and I gave each of them five hundred Rupiah (Indonesian dollars). I started to think about the possibility of their spending the night in a mansion or cruising in a BMW, but dismissed that thought as folly. Then I thought I could have given them too much money. Five hundred Rupiah could have been too much. Because one U.S. dollar equaled ten thousand Rupiah, I actually only gave them a nickel each—not too much at all. After examining my actions, I decided that I probably was doing the right thing, so I decided to continue giving money if the request was repeated.

The following couple of days, I handed out five hundred dollar bills out to each of the ladies who were begging when I would pass their way. By the end of our trip, they would see us coming, stand up, and greet us as we approached. In passing, I mentioned to my friend that the ladies seemed happier for the fact that we were coming by to greet them rather than for the mere fact that I would give them some of my spare change. I said this because towards the end of our trip, the ladies did not ask for money nor did they push their cups or baskets towards me. They only smiled and shook my hand as we walked. My friend responded that they appreciated my placing the money in their hands because not many people like to get close to them. He added that all the lepers in Yogyakarta would probably appreciate that.

Lepers? I knew that is what I heard, but I mentally went through any words that might sound the same—leopards, shepherds, helpers, letters—nope. He definitely said lepers. I stopped walking when I realized what he said. I didn't know lepers were still around. In fact, I never really thought about it, but I figured that leprosy went away with the temple tax or the Roman Empire. I instinctively reached for my Purell hand sanitizer, thinking that it would have been convenient if he had told me about their being lepers upon our arrival as opposed to the day we were leaving town. The whole rest of the day, I walked around different historical sites wondering if I had leprosy and how I was going to explain that to my dad who had expressed concerns about my going in the first place.

As the day wore on, I soon pushed the idea that I might have leprosy to the back of my mind and enjoyed the tour, but used my hand sanitizer at least once every thirty minutes. When we returned to our hotel, we passed only two ladies and they greeted me in the usual fashion. I knew I had to greet them as before and I did, but it was a struggle as I glanced to their hands and faces to see the tell-tale signs of their disease. That night I lay awake for two reasons—I was praying that I did not contract leprosy, and I was also disgruntled with myself. I thought long and hard about touch and how God's touch differed so greatly from mine.

When I didn't know about their infirmities, I treated them as I should and it made a difference. Now that I knew that they were ill, deep within me I didn't want to touch them out of fear for my own personal safety and out of repulsion for the disease. I thought about Christ and how he always seemed to be laying hands on people—and many of those people had communicable diseases.

To top it off, Christ didn't have hand sanitizer or antibiotic cream or health insurance. And yet he still reached out to them. How sad is it that I would withdraw my touch—the touch that gave a sense of acceptance to people who faced banishment for so long—out of selfishness? Why couldn't I be filled with Christ to the point that I do not recoil when I come in contact with fear? How amazing is God's touch that it touches, loves, accepts, and redeems the broken, the diseased, and the hopeless without ever conceiving a thought about personal welfare.

"what's your name?" vs. "Who Are You?"

One of the first things students study in a foreign language class is how to introduce themselves. Some of my students in China had memorized the phrases "How do you do?" and "Fine, thanks. And you?" and loved to use them in conversation. It all worked fine if I started the conversation or if they started the conversation and I didn't ask them how they were doing. We actually went a long time until we found the problem lurking in the dialogue. It went like this:

> Student: "Teacher, how do you do?"
>
> Me: "Fine. How are you?"
>
> Student: "Fine, thanks. And you?"
>
> Me: "Oh, I'm fine. How are you?"

I do remember finally catching on to it, but I have no idea how many times I repeated the beginning of conversations before I realized what was going on. Once I noticed that I was repeating the beginning of conversations, I started to notice that I did it more frequently than I thought possible—and that was a problem.

The problem with our conversations was not so much with learning a foreign language. They had memorized a cute phrase that worked most of the time. Students *were* learning a foreign language. The problem came from me and the other native English speakers—we would greet and respond as if we had memorized the script as well. Even when one of us had a bad day, the response remained the same—"Fine."

As a result of that experience, I ended up trying to really ask how a person was—to ask it expecting a real response. This new method backfired, however, because I somehow ended up asking people "How are you?" at least twice when the first answer seemed too automatic. I am not really sure how I started doing that, but the only result was that people started to think I either was hard of hearing or an idiot. I soon figured out that I needed to stop repeating questions and that it was best to not ask "How are you?" Not that I shouldn't ask how someone was doing, but I should personalize it—if I wanted a personal answer, the question should be personal, too. That makes sense. Instead of asking someone "How are you?" I started to ask how their day at work was or if they had a tough day—just changing the wording—and the responses seemed to change immediately. Soon I found out how people were really doing—how their families were and all of that. I soon felt—and I think everyone else did too—closer to those around me as if we were becoming more intertwined with each other in our experiences.

Since I am somewhat of a language person, I soon wanted to experiment with other parts of our day-to-day greetings. The one thing that popped up was how we ask "Who are you?" or "Who is that?" If asked, "What is your name?" the answer is simple. However, if someone asks, "Who are you?" well that is a much more involved question. "Who am I?" is made up of who I was, how I was brought up, what I believe, and many other things. Of course, the only reply we give is our name—if we gave more, people would probably start thinking that we were a little off our rockers. In my head though, it made lots of sense. Imagine the following conversation:

Student: "Teacher, what is your name?"

Me: "Thomas Herrington. What is your name?"

Student: "Guang Ping."

Me: "Nice to meet you, Guang Ping."

Student: "Nice to meet you, too."

That is the run of the mill conversation—but what if it were like this:

Student: "Excuse me, we haven't met. Who are you?"

Me: "I am the son of Robert and Mary Herrington. I am a Christian. I am an American and I am a dreamer. My name is Thomas."

Student: "Nice to meet you. You are really, really strange…"

I knew that a greeting would never survive a response like that, even though it answered the question better than just a name, so fearing that I would become a social outcast, I begrudgingly gave up that peculiar reply and stayed with the accepted patterns of speech.

Although I gave up on my idea for revolutionizing greetings, I didn't stop thinking about the question "Who are you?" That is a huge question. As Americans, we often fail in answering this question because our culture leads us to think what we do defines us. A definition of *self* based on what one can do and/or his accomplishments leaves a person in a precarious position because jobs and physical abilities are far from being constant. And in our Christian walk, what does that mean? If I say I am a Christian—that should define who I am, but often times it is more of a label than an all-encompassing way of life.

So exactly who are we? Who are we to become? To know truly who we are, we must recognize what we were, who we are now, and what we aim to become. If I say I am a teacher, well, that means I am only "me" Monday through Friday. On Saturdays and Sundays, I would have to redefine who I am because I do not teach on those days since teaching isn't a constant in my life, and it doesn't define who I am. If that is so, then perhaps what is constant in my life defines who I am. With that thought in mind, I made a list of constants—Christian, American, Mississippian, upper-lower-middle class, husband of Marni Herrington, son of Robert and Mary Herrington, brother of Ramsey Herrington, allergic to a lot of things, short attention span, Cherry Coke drinker, hater of scary movies, and creative. These things are constant—and there are many more things that are constant—but all of them do not define who I am. So if all constants do not define who I am, what does?

Perhaps to understand who we are, we must remember where we came from, who we are now, and who we are to become. To get to who we are now, we need to first see who we were. Two good examples of people who didn't forget who they were and as a result managed to keep who they were in perspective were John the Baptist and "the sinful woman."[48] Sometimes it is hard to forget where we came from because people won't let you. For instance, "Rahab the Harlot" and "the sinful woman" will always be known as such. At least Rahab got her name in the Bible. "The sinful woman" just has the label. These were the kind of women that everyone gossiped about at PTA meetings.

At the opposite end of the spectrum was John the Baptist. He was righteous, but he was a nut. He lived in the wilderness and wore handmade clothes from animal hides. He was the kind of guy everybody made fun of in third grade because he dressed funny and didn't have a fancy Trapper-Keeper or a new, fancy pair of shoes. And yet what? People were drawn to him. In droves people came to hear this eccentric man. Why? Both John and "the sinful woman" knew, truly knew who Jesus was—and therefore knew who they were. As a result, their names are immortalized in the Bible as examples of true devotion.

John basically got a team together, gave them a purpose, did great things, reached the championship game, and someone said, "Oh, yeah. The coach is here to replace you." And what did John do? He said, "Okay," stated that he wasn't worthy to take off Jesus' sandals and left only to be beheaded. Who in his right mind would do something like that? John the Baptist did all of the preaching, baptizing, and leading. Those were *his* followers. Those were *his* friends, followers, and enemies; all of him was used up to get to where he was at that moment. Then he gave it all away. His whole life, given up. Why? He never forgot who he was because he never forgot who he was following.

Why would a woman who did everything that she should not, bust up into a religious leader's house to commit the most selfless act? A religious leader who would gladly stone this woman if he caught her near a gravel pit, the man who made her feel completely worthless, the man who made her feel as empty as she had become, a man who she surely loathed; she would surely cringe at the mention of his name. That is whose house she barged into. She went in to make a fool of herself. Why? Because in the house of the man who hated her the most and condemned who she was, sat a man who loved her more than anything and gladly would forgive who she was; just as he would gladly help her become who she ought to be. She had messed up—she knew who she was, but she knew who Jesus was. That was enough.

To find who they were in Jesus was enough to drive a man into the wilderness to find God and enough for a woman to leave the only life she had ever known, just for a glimmer of hope. In the pious and the broken, we find the same answer resounding—we define who we are in Jesus Christ. And in knowing Him, we see that we are unworthy. Despite a near perfect performance by John the Baptist and an imperfect performance by "the sinful woman," we see that they, in their unworthiness, reacted to a holy God's glory and gladly yielded to His will.

To know that we are unworthy is a start, but to discover who we are now, we need to look at another person in the Bible. Paul never forgot who he was. He was "the man." Reading about the life of Paul, it seems that he should have been a pope, president, or dictator. He was "it." He knew that within the confines of the law, he was right. He even attacked those who didn't hold the same beliefs. As a Jew, he did it all, he did it right, and he did it with zeal.

138 — *Thomas Herrington*

And yet, Paul talked a lot about grace. He knew that if it weren't for grace, there would be no hope in life. Why? He realized who he was—when he looked at Jesus and then himself, it was easy to see sinfulness, impurity, short-comings, etc. The same is with us. If you want to feel good about yourself, just compare yourself to someone worse than you. You will always be able to find someone worse, more sinful, more evil, not as giving, someone who doesn't go to Sunday School all the time, someone who double-parks, or goes farther than you would in a relationship. But with Jesus, there are no shadows to hide in, no stumbling blocks to hide behind. Compared to perfection, the "almost perfect" loses its appeal rapidly. And what must be done when you come to the realization that who you are isn't who you should be? You change.

For example, when I was little, I always believed I could die for Christ. There were many Cold War stories of Christians dying for their beliefs and the stories made me daydream about being able to do the same. What I didn't realize is that in a south Mississippi town, it is easy to say that I would die for Christ because the closest I could get to dying for the church is if I were to choke on some chicken during the Wednesday night supper. Nonetheless, I liked to think of myself as a possible martyr, with the backbone and faith that would allow me to follow until the bitter end. This all changed, however, when I read *Through Gates of Splendor*, the book about Jim Elliot, Ed McCully, Nate Saint, Pete Fleming, and Roger Youderian, missionaries who were killed while sharing with Auca Indians in the jungles of Ecuador. The book I bought had pictures—I love books with pictures and could always tell when a book had photos because the page edges were a little darker than the rest. I flipped open the book, thinking "woohoo, pictures" and saw a nice photo of Jim and his friends smiling. Other photos were of the missionaries' families. And then, there it was—a photograph of a missionary, dead, floating in the river with a spear protruding from his torso. He was dead. Dead. That word seemed so heavy. I couldn't keep from looking at the book. Finally, I had to put it down because right then I realized that I couldn't do that. The cost was too high. Why couldn't I die for God? Because I wasn't dead to myself. If I'm not dead to self, I am not going to die to anyone else. If I am dead to myself, then there is nothing else to lose.

What do we need to do when we find out who we are isn't who we thought we were? Or when we find out who we are isn't who we should be? We change.

How much change depends on the individual. It is sort of like speeding and seeing a police car. It doesn't matter which lane you are in, what you are driving, or what engagement you are rushing off to; if you are speeding, well, you are just that—speeding. You slow down to a uniform speed—the one set before you. The faster you are going, the more drastic a change is needed. The same with Christ—he is set before us as a canon for our lives. Some people will have to make bigger lifestyle changes than others, but no matter how big or small, change is still needed. Jesus set the bar high through living his life, and we are prompted forward with the creed "Be holy as your father in heaven is holy."

Along with who we are and what we are doing, what we want changes with where we are in life. So if we can solidify who we are and where we are, then what we want will start to solidify as well. For instance, a friend of mine and I would have to drive from Jackson, Mississippi, to Memphis, Tennessee, and back on occasion. Often these trips would take place in one day and the time spent in Memphis would often be less than the time spent in the car. While on those trips, I would mention that it would be really nice to have a helicopter. But I don't drive to Memphis all of the time, so a helicopter wouldn't be that handy. While commuting to and from work, I am glad I drive what I do, and even though my car doesn't have a tail rotor or a collective pitch stick, it still drinks plenty of gasoline. So when I am putting gas in it, I start to think, *Hmm, it would be nice to drive a scooter or an electric car.*

That is the same way it is with my spiritual life. All the time, I would pray, "God, where are you? I can't hear you. Draw me close. Renew me. Fill me up." But I never changed what I was doing. I still wouldn't find time for a quiet time. When I did, it would be rushed and without direction. Since I never changed, the void remained and the prayers stayed the same: "God, where are you? I can't hear you. Draw me close. Renew me. Fill me up." Since I am a little slow at times, it took me a while to figure out that for a change to take place, I had to stop wallowing in complacency and do something about my stagnant spirituality. And what should I do? How should I change? Not by going out and doing things, learning a new praise song, or buying a new Christian t-shirt, but by truly humbling myself out of the realization that I am unworthy and God is almighty.

To truly realize that God is great—to see a glimpse of how holy he truly is—should drive us to humility and leave us bowing at his feet. When we come to him, we should come as the lesser—the one who is grateful to have an opportunity to worship—and find that God is greater. John the Baptist said that "He must become greater and I must become less." This is coming from the guy who gave up everything—family, possessions, success, popularity—he was in jail and still said, "I must become less. He must become greater." John never forgot who he was and, therefore, knew what he was to become.

When we find ourselves in a position where we have to change, what do we do next? What can we do, or what should we do? The first thing is to realize that we can't "do" our way into Heaven. We are "not competent in ourselves," but that "competence comes from God." Recognize who we are—sinful, separated from God, and that we are to become like Christ. Be so like Christ, that we can "rejoice in suffering" for him and not think twice about being poured out like a "drink offering." Take the phrase "to live is Christ, to die is gain." Replace "Christ" with anything else, and you get "loss." To live is to be successful, to die is loss. To live is to be popular, to die is loss. Only Christ, in his fullness, goes beyond the grave to allow us to gain in his wonderful, complete glory.

So why live, sold out, striving for what you can become? Why strive to be like-minded with Christ? What happens when we leave who we are behind to find our identity in Christ? Take Daniel (Belteshazzar), Shadrach, Meshach, and Abednego for example. What did they do that made them different, sold out to God? For one thing, they ate their vegetables. For others, they did not put God in second place. What happened? A fiery furnace and a lion's den.

King Nebuchadnezzar had a dream and he couldn't remember it, but it sure had him worried. He wanted someone to tell him the dream that he had dreamt and had promptly forgotten. And then he wanted them to tell him what it meant. What? A king declares, "Tell me what I forgot, the dream you can't possibly know, then interpret it, or I will cut you to pieces." That is like a math teacher saying, "I forgot the word problem, but something is traveling from somewhere at some speed. Tell me when it would get to Topeka, Kansas or I'll give you an 'F' and you won't pass four-year-old kindergarten." Impossible. It was an impossible task, but for God "all things are possible."

Why Daniel? Was it that he had a doctorate in dream interpretation or that he was the recipient of various accolades? He probably didn't even get "most likely to succeed" or "wittiest" in his high school annual. But he would have gotten the "will realize who he is because of an encounter with God and will see that who he is isn't where he should be, so he will gladly forsake every plan, dream, and hope that he ever had just because he would rather be known as a vessel or tool for God's use rather than receive anything that this world has to offer" award—if, of course, the award was up for grabs.

And what difference did Daniel's devotion make? So what if a guy follows something whole-heartedly? The difference he made is this: a king who worshipped pagan gods, a man so morally deteriorated that he would kill all of his wise men because they could not perform the impossible, fell "prostrate before Daniel and paid him honor and ordered that an offering and incense be presented to him." He then said to Daniel, "surely your God is the God of gods and the Lord of kings, and a revealer of mysteries, for you were able to reveal this mystery." The guy that everyone made fun of for eating his broccoli and spinach rather than eating a steak; that dweeby guy that isn't man enough to drink like the rest of the king's workers; yeah, that guy has a king on his face in front of him, because through Daniel, that king saw a glimpse of what the Almighty God is like.

That glimpse changes people. It changes their perspectives, their worries, fears, hopes, dreams, wants, joys, ambitions—all are changed because one person said, "God, who you are is what I want to emulate; I'm not there yet, but with my eyes on You, I'm running hard and I'm running straight."

Sure, Daniel could do it, but how about us? We are trying to change, but it isn't easy. Does Christ know that it isn't easy? Yeah. He was there. He was there when the crowds walked away. He was there when his own creation rejected him. He even knew that sometimes he wasn't going to win. He said that "John the Baptist came neither eating bread nor drinking wine and you say, 'he has a demon.' The Son of Man came eating and drinking, and you say, 'Here is a glutton and a drunkard, a friend of tax-collectors and sinners.'" He knows that people aren't perfect—and that is one of the reasons He chose to be called the "Lion of Judah."

So who is Judah? Have you ever wondered why Christ was the "Lion of Judah" and not someone else? I think part of the reason is this: Judah messed up. Why? Because people aren't perfect. God is perfect and with every interaction with God, God will try to bring us closer to him, which in turn, brings us closer to perfection.

Judah, trying to uphold the law, tried to get his son Onan to marry the widow of Er, Judah's first born. They did this in order to produce an heir. Well, Onan didn't do what he should. He died. So Judah moved the widow into his house. Her name was Tamar and, well, she wanted a son. She heard that Judah would be traveling (he had been widowed by this point), so she dressed up like a prostitute and waited for Judah. Judah saw her and wished to purchase her services. He didn't have any cash and there wasn't an ATM nearby, so he left her his jacket as collateral. Thinking that she was going to wait for him, he rushed off into town and on the way back, grabbed some money for his payment. On the way back, however, she wasn't there. Later, Judah returned home only to find out that Tamar was pregnant. He still didn't know that she was the prostitute. That is important to the plot of the story. Well, Judah, thought, "what kind of nasty, good-for-nothing are you? I invited you in my house and now you are sleeping around with God knows who!" So Judah took Tamar outside, called out everybody to maximize the shame of Tamar, and wanted a vote for burning her to death. About this time, Tamar cleared her throat and announced, "Yeah, I've been a really bad girl, but see if you can tell me who the father is by this." At that, she whipped out Judah's college letterman jacket and there, embroidered on the left side of the jacket in large letters for everyone to read was "JUDAH."

Needless to say, Judah's plan backfired. Instead of being looked upon as pious, righteous, with a daughter-in-law punished for her shameful deeds, he was embarrassed, exposed, and caught red-handed in something that would make the local paper's headlines. It probably read the next day—"Local man has son/grandson from prostitute/daughter-in-law" right above the photo of Tamar waving Judah's jacket in the air, glad she had a "get-out-of-jail-free" card. Poor Judah. He messed up. We mess up. We all need God. We all need to draw closer to God.

Jesus knows it's hard. He used Judah as his representative. Why would he do that? He wants us to know that there will be days when we fall; but he will be there waiting to pick us up, cleanse our wounds, wipe our tears, and make us whole again. All of that if we just let him. What are we waiting for? He knows who we are. Isn't it time to know who we are by getting to know who he really is?

bread and
Water

Growing up, I can honestly say that I never knew what the word "need" meant. I used the word often, and still do on occasion, but as for what it truly meant, I was in the dark.

Even though I can't really grasp what that word means, I use it often in language. I enjoy using extremes in language and do not care for moderation when it comes to emotion. I hate movies or I love them. I am starving by ten past twelve and I am dying to see photos of my friend's new significant other. I will kill him or her for standing me up when we had an appointment, and I will call someone an idiot, moron, or imbecile if he makes the slightest mistake. If I work too hard at my job, I am not overworked, but I am a slave and my boss is a slave driver. A girl who makes a poor decision is labeled a whore, and a guy who overreacts to something is psycho or crazy. And yet, after September 2005, these titles wavered when the reality that I live in was shaken and some of the most basic things were taken away from my family.

On a late Thursday night, I drove down to Columbia. I stopped to meet up with a friend in Hattiesburg and then we drove to our parents' homes, which were only days before ravaged by Hurricane Katrina. In our two vehicles, we had over eighty gallons of water, three generators, one propane stove, thirty bags of ice, and loads of other things because our parents and their friends *needed* these items. We drove into our town wary of the local population who looted several stores and also wary of the local law enforcement who were, under martial law, allowed to shoot first without the usual protocols. For this trip to happen, we had to carry extra gasoline for the return trip and phone the police. The authorities even recommended we accept a police escort to my friend's mother's home to ensure our safety. It truly did not feel like going home.

Upon our arrival to Columbia, I met my parents at my home. They were sleeping on the floor in an attempt to escape the oppressive heat, leaving the windows open at night hoping a breeze would break the stagnant, thick, humid air. My father moved through the house that was so quiet, it whispered secrets about the hell that had taken place there. My mother also came to meet me at the door, her matted hair and shiny complexion showed that the water was not working and had not worked for several days. I only brought them a portion of what my friend and I brought down—simple things like water, orange juice, milk, ice, bread, peanut butter, and jelly. Simple things that fill every shelf in every home. Simple things that are cheap, common, and often not thought about. Simple things. My mother cried.

Before September, I didn't know a life that had bread lines, gas lines, and pure desperation. The stories my grandfather would tell of waiting in breadlines during the Great Depression or how my father only ate three times a week during college were so distant that they seemed unrealistic. Hunger never was at my elbow, but rather hunger and starvation were just terms applied to other countries or were used for exaggeration. Never had a friend asked if I owned a handgun, and if I did, please bring it for safety as we traveled home. Never had I known a world to exist where credit cards were not accepted and stores ran out of food. Never had I seen people waiting for three hours to get gas, even when they were told the gas station would only serve medical professionals. Never had I tried to call family members for days on end and not be able to get through. Never had I seen a mother cry when given bread and water. My mother cried.

Something within me changed. It was something that was not supposed to happen, like when a parent outlives his child; something unnatural intervenes in the relationship. So it was with me when I, the child, came to the aid of my parents, the ones who were needy. Now when I see my parents, I have this thing within my chest, dwelling, almost wanting to explode—some emotion that I have never felt before—almost as if my parents and I swapped roles for a few days. I felt like, for an instant, that I were they. And they were I. To give to them, in their need, their *need*—how that word cannot pack the true weight of it all—and then to realize that I am nothing but a child. Some bond that I didn't know could exist welled up inside of me and made me feel closer, stronger, weaker, and more responsible to my parents.

I am not sure what will happen from here, what the next storm will look like, or how long it will take for my hometown to rebuild. I don't know if people will really change after the storm, or if they will go back to living life as if the disaster never happened. I am not sure if I will not use the word "need" for "want" or if I will use the word "starve" for "hungry." I do know that I want to change.

I do know that when I see bread and water, when I see my mother and father, when I hear their voices, then I am grateful. My hope and prayer is that I never forget. That I never lose that connection, that bond that I share with my parents. I hope that with every day, every meal, every night when all is well, I can remember that through the fury of the hurricane and the destruction wrought, my family not only survived, but they are able to give thanks together on a newer, higher level. And know that there is a reason. There is a reason that my mother cried.

no more
Moo Goo

The Great Wall Chinese restaurant menu in Clinton, Mississippi, lists over a hundred names of different dishes—moo goo gai pan, sub gum wo ba, chicken chow mein, and shrimp lo mein. The menu looks like a random group of letters fell on the pages with the occasional chicken, beef, or shrimp in the middle. Despite the menu at the Great Wall not yielding many clues to what different dishes are, I still go to this little hole in the wall restaurant. Three of us, Melvin, Thomas McGill and I, darken the door of that little restaurant any time all three of us are in Clinton at the same time. For less than seven bucks, a customer can buy two canned Cokes and more food than a person could ever hope to eat in one sitting.

My wife, on the other hand, likes the big Chinese buffets—the ones that brag because they have over fifty yards of buffet and every animal that isn't on an endangered species list. This preference is not because she loves to gorge herself on Chinese food, but for the opposite reason: she doesn't like Chinese food. She likes the big buffets because she can find French fries, macaroni and cheese, pizza, and other foods that resemble "all-American" food and can dodge the imitation crab sushi or the beef and broccoli stir fry.

My wife is not alone in her dislike for Chinese food. Lots of people in the United States do not like it, and they all have similar excuses—"It is always in a sauce," "I don't like everything mixed in together," "too sweet," "too salty," "there might be dog or cat meat in there," etc.

My wife is a trooper, however. Even though she dislikes Chinese food, she agreed to go to China with me one summer. Due to her dislike of the food, I had no idea how the trip would go, but we managed. Granted we ate at McDonalds, Pizza Hut, and KFC more during that one week than I had in the previous six months, but we did eat Chinese food as well. While in Beijing, my former roommate and his fiancée met up with us, and we ate a good Chinese meal. Being polite, my wife tried one of the dishes and found out that she really liked it. She liked it enough to recommend that we order it again. To me that was a great victory. That day, I thought it was a little odd that my wife would like Chinese food in China when she didn't like the "Americanized" version in Oxford, but I soon remembered my own food aversions. I don't like Mexican food. I say that, but I soon found out that I didn't like "Mexican food in Oxford."

On a mission trip to Mexico, our group spent a full week doing construction projects and street evangelism. Our fearless group leader, Elizabeth Scaife, didn't want us eating at chain restaurants, but she rather found us little hole-in-the-wall restaurants where we partook in *real* Mexican food. It was great. I still wasn't the biggest fan of cilantro, but the Mexican food that I ate on the patio of some little run-down Matamoras café was the best Mexican food I had tasted in my life. Upon my return, I thought, *Oh, boy, let's go to the local "El whatever" and have a run of tacos and enchiladas.* It was slightly disappointing, because it wasn't like it was in Mexico, but the good part about it was that I could appreciate *real* Mexican food even more because I knew how good it was and how hard it must be to crank out authentic Mexican food in Oxford, Mississippi, a town that isn't a great bastion of diversity.

The tragedy isn't that I think Mexican food is better in Mexico or that my wife doesn't really like going to *China Moon* or *Golden Dragon*. The real tragedy is when individuals go to Mexico or

China and do not eat the food there because they don't like it in their hometown.

On my travels, I have met many people who do this—these are often the people you see eating three meals a day at an American chain restaurant while staying in Lima or Bangkok or any other city. And for those travelers who esteem food a part of culture that they want to experience, this antipathy towards foreign cuisine seems ridiculous and tragic, but all in all not much is lost—all they are missing out on is a good meal.

A tragedy of epic proportions is that all around us there are individuals who do the same thing with church. They have had a taste of the local church or perhaps they just saw a Christian having a bad day and decided that wasn't what they wanted. God is awesome and perfect—and when people see the slightest bit of imperfection within the church, they walk away not ever wanting to go back. If a person talks much about religion in the United States, one of the things he will most likely hear as a complaint is hypocrisy in the church. I am sure that the pastor's wife double-parked or that one of the deacons honked his horn getting impatient in traffic. Even worse things have been done by those in church leadership and witnessed by those outside the church—but these imperfections are just that—imperfections. The local window of heaven, the church, isn't perfect, but that shouldn't prevent people from realizing that heaven is and God is so much better and bigger than all that is here. To allow superficial imperfections to prevent people from experiencing true worship—people's true purpose—that is the greatest tragedy of all.

If you have found yourself slacking with church or have quit altogether because of a negative run-in with someone at the church, remember that people aren't what the church is to be about. It is about God, his worship, and his purposes. And when you run out of reasons to go back or you are having a hard time dragging yourself out of bed, know this—Jesus experienced the same thing.

Jesus spent hours and hours at the temple—at the temple where the people didn't understand him, wanted to stone him, and eventually bought off one of his closest friends to betray him. And yet when Jesus spoke about the temple, he never defamed it, and he never tried to stop people from going to it. The Pharisees and Sadducees had to get on his nerves for being so hypocritical and prideful and yet Jesus taught his disciples to do what they say. He told them to do all that the leaders of the law told them—to "do and observe, but do not do according to their deeds."[49]

Jesus had a following and knew more about the scriptures than anyone around. He could have caused a split in the church, fussed at a business meeting, and talked behind someone's back until a new temple was formed and he was the new pastor. He could have, but he didn't. Jesus told his disciples to not only keep going, but to listen to what the teachers said—to ignore their hypocrisy and acknowledge that the word of God is still the word of God regardless of who repeats it.

If you have been turned off to church and/or what God is doing because of others who have misrepresented the word and the example of Christ, I hope that you find the strength and motivation to heed the words of Christ—to obey God and to find fellowship with fellow believers.

meal-dependent exercise-induced
Cholinergic Urticaria

Growing up, I always had to struggle with allergies. I didn't really have extreme allergies to hay or crustaceans or what-have-you—my allergy was and still is due to the combination of food and heat. If I eat right after I have been exercising or if I eat and then go for a bike ride, I will have an allergic reaction. As a result of this allergy, I have made many emergency room visits, carry Benadryl in my pocket almost incessantly, and on long trips I pack an Epi-Pen "just in case."

My first bad allergic reaction was when I was in second grade. We had eaten supper and went for a walk around the block as we normally would. This time, however, I brought a tennis ball. As opposed to the usual, leisurely walk around the neighborhood, I threw the tennis ball as high as I could and then chased it as it bounced down the street. By the time we made it half-way around the block, I started to complain because I was itching all over. By the time my parents got me to our house, my allergic reaction was so severe that they rushed me to the hospital to get medical help.

Not too long after that, I had another allergic reaction at a birthday party. At first, the doctors thought my allergic reaction was due to a spider bite then perhaps I was allergic to tomatoes. Time after time, they could not pinpoint the reason for my allergic reactions. After trips to almost every pediatric clinic in the Southeast, my diagnosis came through—I had *Meal-Dependent Exercise-Induced Cholinergic Urticaria*, which, as a child, was pretty cool to say and impossible to spell.

Soon most of my friends and their parents knew I had this allergy. Most were curious about how I could be allergic to all food if I were hot, but most just watched me closely at birthday parties. Parents would try to protect me either by not feeding me or making me sit down for two hours after I ate.

The problems came, surprisingly, at Wednesday night church. We would eat supper and then go to Royal Ambassadors. My mother would go to choir practice, and my dad would go to a Bible study. Without adult supervision (sometimes I would skip RAs) or when the RA leader would take us to the gym before the Bible study, the problems would come. My inconspicuous, Wednesday night supper would turn into a villain that made me get rushed to the hospital to receive a shot of epinephrine and shake for the next two hours because I was not disciplined enough to not play with my friends.

As an elementary school student, I found waiting patiently for two hours to pass was nearly impossible. I would go to the gym with the intent of just watching. After a while, I would think, *Oh, I will just shoot the basketball. No running.* And before you knew it, I was running all over the place playing a scrimmage game with friends until I started itching. Then I would have to repeat the whole "trip to the hospital, get a shot, shake" routine.

Due to my lack of maturity, my inability to sit still, and my lack of self-discipline, Wednesday night meals tried to kill me. At friends' birthday parties, parents soon learned to keep me away from the food, made me a to-go plate, or just tied me down after eating because they knew I couldn't muster up the discipline to say "no" to the next kick ball game or game of tag. And for the parents that did adjust, it took a lot of effort on their part.

Anytime my friends' parents had me over as a guest, it was second nature for them to offer me food and drink. Countless times, a group of friends would show up at a house and the mother would offer milk, Cokes, cookies, or ice cream and then have to add "except for Thomas." Then they would eye me as if they were trying to determine whether or not I was mature enough to eat and then wait my two hours. And they always ended up feeding everyone but me, so I figure they thought I wouldn't make it. So parents learned and my friends learned, which was odd for them because they could eat and play as they pleased and not be affected. Eventually I learned, too.

Living with my odd allergy, I found out that sometimes what is okay for the majority may not be okay for a few. A lack of self-discipline or a circumstance out of their control may make what is harmless into something dangerous. This is a condition that existed in the early church and persists even today. In Paul's letter to the church in Corinth, he addressed a similar problem. Through Christ's freedom, many people were eating food offered to idols, which didn't bother them because they knew that idols weren't real and that through Christ they had a newfound freedom. Some, however, didn't handle this new freedom very well. Perhaps it was because they were not used to having the freedom, or it could be because they were devout idol worshippers in the past—no one knows—but we do know that some in the church were struggling with others' eating food given to idols and that others didn't have a problem partaking of the food. Paul wrote:

> Take care that this liberty of yours does not somehow become a stumbling block to the weak. For if someone sees you, who have knowledge, dining in an idol's temple, will not his conscience, if he is weak, be strengthened to eat things sacrificed to idols? For through your knowledge he who is weak is ruined, the brother for whose sake Christ died. And so, by sinning against the brethren and wounding their conscience when it is weak, you sin against Christ. Therefore, if food causes my brother to stumble, I will never eat meat again, so that I will not cause my brother to stumble.[50]

This isn't a fun verse. No one likes to give up freedoms. My friends didn't want to give up their snack time because I couldn't eat, but some did, and I appreciated their help in my struggle with my allergies. The same goes for a friend who may be struggling with alcoholism—if you forego the drink at dinner, you would keep the temptation out of reach of your friend, and you would help him in his struggle.

But how? Why? If Christ gave us freedoms, why should we give up these freedoms? Why can't they just learn to cope with their own problems? Paul knew that these questions would arise—and that is why he finished his statement by saying he would not eat meat at all if that would keep his brothers from stumbling. He also knew that those trying to give up these freedoms to help others needed a reason for doing so. Before he started his argument, he covered some background knowledge that the readers already. As a result, he started by saying "Knowledge makes people arrogant but love edifies."[51] I can hear the echoes of arguments he no doubt had in and around temples.

"You shouldn't eat that. It is for the idols, and idols are for the pagans."

"Well, I don't think the statue is gonna mind that I took his food. It is just gonna rot here anyways…"

"What happens if Ole Man Marley sees you doing this? He may start to think it is okay to come in here—he doesn't know you are just coming in for free food and that you aren't worshipping."

"Well, what do you say we ask the statue over here—um, statue, if you object to me taking this food, please say something. If not, please remain silent. And if Mr. Marley comes in, please tell him all we did was get food."

"Funny. Real funny."

Through one's knowledge that the idols are powerless, a person could consume food offered to idols without guilt or without worry. The problem was that the knowledge did not allow many people to have compassion on others who might struggle with idol worship and disregarded their weakness in light of their own strengths.

In verses two through six,[52] Paul outlines this knowledge—that, yes, there is only one God and there is no reason to worry about idols. Through his letter, Paul told the early believers that they weren't wrong in their actions when they were eating meat offered to idols—they were wrong in their hearts. And even the slightest glance towards who God is will find that God is more interested in the hearts of men than in their actions. And, no matter how inconvenient it may be, we are supposed to yield. We are to give up that which is a freedom to prevent others around us from stumbling. And if all of that isn't enough reason to deter you from doing something, whatever it may be, that leads others to stumble, remember the verse, "Do unto others as you would have them do unto you." Stumbling isn't fun for the stumbling—and when we are falling, we would want help and reinforcement as well.

Remember, we do have freedom—but Christ intends for us to use our freedom to help our brothers and sisters as opposed to serving ourselves.

"m.c. hammer pants" and
Clip-On Ties

My parents are faithful church-goers. Even when we were on vacation in some unknown town, we would find a church to go to on Sunday morning. My father would check out the yellow pages and decide on a church and then ask some bystander how to reach such-and-such address and then our family would be off to the unknown.

There is something else you should know about my family—we are perpetually late for everything. This means that our family van would break every state traffic regulation that existed to reach a serene house of worship. It also means that we couldn't just come in and have a seat, but rather we made a big entrance because the service always was well under way upon our arrival, and my dad didn't like to sit in the back but rather front and center. Another thing you should know about my family is that we always forgot something. Well, actually I always forgot something. Something as in socks or shoes or a tie or what-have-you (or all of the above). In fact, I packed knowing I would forget something and still could not prevent it from happening.

One particular trip, we were vacationing in Townsend, Tennessee, the self-proclaimed "peaceful side" of the Smoky Mountains. My father choosing this destination for a family vacation is not uncommon because over half of our family vacations ended up in

Townsend. My father's idea of a vacation does not include traffic or more than a thousand people, so anything proclaiming itself as quiet or peaceful had an immediate pull on our vacation destinations. While we were staying at a hotel in Townsend, my father once again planned to make an excursion to church where we would brave the halls of a new place to spend our Sunday morning. He found a church that he liked from the church's name and hiked down to the nearest restaurant to get directions.

When dad got back to the hotel room, he told us the time we would leave and to make sure we had everything before Sunday morning. In my efforts to make sure I was ready, I started taking inventory. That Saturday night I made the discovery that I remembered to bring socks (they were the usual culprit), but I did forget to bring a pair of dress pants. Since my parents didn't want me to wear jeans to church and especially not shorts, my parents said that they would pick up something at K-Mart that night. Something in my mind should have told me to go with them, but I opted to stay and play in the pool—an error that I would not repeat.

The next morning, when I began to get ready for church, my mother presented me with my new "Sunday clothes." The most psychedelic pair of pants with neon green, pink, and yellow were stretched out to me, and I just stared at my mom as if she were crazy.

"I can't go to church wearing M.C. Hammer pants," I complained.

"I thought you would like them. You mean you don't like them?" I kept staring at my mom. This is the same lady that made me wear a suit to Sunday night church when everyone else was wearing shorts and t-shirts. I made a mental note that if I had problems later in life that I should blame it on this emotionally scarring Sunday morning.

"Mom… the churches up here only play songs with the same instruments on the 'Deliverance' soundtrack. This isn't going to be good…"

"Just hurry up. We are going to be late."

"And I still can't wear jeans? Jeans are better than those. I promise. Please?" Mom looked at me with her "do-we-need-to-go-over-this-again" look, and I knew right then and there I wasn't going to convince her into letting me wear jeans, so I sulkingly grabbed the pants and put them on. MC Hammer pants really aren't that bad when they are worn with a matching shirt and shoes, but they really stood out with my short-sleeved light blue button-up shirt, clip-on tie, and dress shoes.

The actual church service didn't really stand out to me—I was constantly preoccupied with the fact that I looked like the bottom half of me should bust out singing *Can't Touch This* while the top half could carry on with *Just As I Am*. I walked into the church, squished in between my parents as if I had on no pants at all, and scooted down the pew and commenced covering up my lap with my Bible and any spare hymnals lying around. What really frustrated me was not that my brother enjoyed this moment for all it was worth, but rather that my parents really didn't think that it was anything out of the ordinary. Before the last note in the invitation finished resonating through that little country church, I bolted out to our van to hide behind the back doors, cursing my luck that my mom always locked the doors wherever we went. I ran away out of my personal embarrassment, not because of ridicule.

Despite the fact that I was dressed like I was on drugs, the people in the church didn't point it out nor did they stare. That was a far cry from my mental images of the congregation guffawing at my eclectic wardrobe or trying to stone me because they thought I was possessed. I found out in that little country church—where I created the greatest amount of contrast—that I was welcome to come and worship. In a little church that did without an organ, but used banjos, tambourines, and dreadnaught guitars, I was accepted despite my hip-hop pants. That church exhibited an attitude that I doubt I would have repeated if the roles were reversed.

The lesson I learned was simple—Christ doesn't have a dress code. It makes sense—if Christ cared about clothes, I am sure John the Baptist wouldn't have filled the role of the one sent to prepare the way.

In Christ's teachings to the Pharisees, he called them hypocrites because they were more concerned about the outside of the cup and the dish as opposed to the inside of the cup.[53] This was not a new notion found only in the New Testament. At the calling of David, Samuel is reminded that God doesn't look at the outward appearances, but rather God looks at the heart of man.[54]

The desire to judge a book by its cover is commonplace and easy to do. Since the exterior of people is the first thing we see, it is convenient to place judgment upon the person based upon outward characteristics. A judgmental attitude is especially noticed by visitors coming into a church congregation for the first time. I have heard countless people state that they didn't feel welcome at a church because of what they wore or how they looked when they entered the door. How ashamed we should truly become if we were to find out that our judgment of a person's clothes or hair turned away a person from God. James, the half-brother of Jesus, wrote a rather scathing report in his letter to those who were practicing such hypocrisy in the church. He admonished the readers to not become judges among themselves because through judging others, they blasphemed the name by which they were called.[55]

Thinking of that little country church and of their welcoming me in a truly loving manner as opposed to the shallow fascination with surface appearances that is ever-present in our culture, I saw a little glimpse of how Christ would have us welcome those to him. I hope that my church can become like that—and I hope that I can as well. Not a forced "I-know-this-is-what-I-should-do" welcome, but a genuine welcome that is from the overflow of a heart that remembers when it was welcomed by a loving Savior.

accountability and the
Art of Dieting

My wife recently decided to start a diet. Her sister had a lot of success with Weight Watchers (she earned multiple gold stars) and as a result, my wife wanted to see if that plan would work for her. She collected all of the literature that Weight Watchers had to offer and read about what was required of her. She tried to explain it to me, and it sounded about as easy to figure out as learning stock options and being a day trader. She had a certain number of points and she could invest those points into different meals and couldn't spend more than she had, but she also was allotted an additional number of points per week to keep as a reserve or to plan a splurge. The only detailed thing I remember about it is that she was upset with me because men got to have more points than women, and she thought that was rather unfair, if not evidence of gender-bias.

As soon as she received her book, we headed off to the grocery store to find meals and snacks that would help her keep within her point margin, and as we checked out, we discovered that "healthy" food must be a more prized commodity than "junk" food. I started to think there was a conspiracy to kill off everyone who didn't have plentiful financial resources by making "health-food" expensive and junk-food extremely cheap. I kept reassuring myself that this was going to be okay, and I encouraged my wife in her efforts, secretly enjoying the idea that all of the Cokes in the refrigerator would end up being mine.

After the first few days of her diet, things started changing. We started cooking more and quit eating out. In fact, we ceased eating fast food completely. Not only was she going to lose weight, she would increase her lifespan. I found myself changing my habits as well—I didn't want to drink four or five Cokes during the day because I knew that she wanted one, and it probably wasn't nice for me to guzzle down mine in front of her. It was also a little embarrassing to know that we needed to buy a new case of Cokes because of me. Only me. I also found out that the Weight Watchers snacks and the 100 calorie packs are actually really good.

Before I knew it, my diet had changed; I cut down on Cokes, ate healthier, and actually lost ten pounds—all of this without really trying. The reason I did all of that was because the person closest to me started to change and as a result, the change in me was automatic.

If a co-worker started a diet, the results would not have been the same. Even though my co-worker and I would share the same building and perhaps the same goals, we lacked the closeness that served as motivation for me. My wife and I are so close that what one wants and receives affects the other. We are yoked together—and when she changed her course, it changed my course. Sure, I could have yanked back, declared that I really didn't care and was going to eat all of the fast food I wanted until I needed a new set of Carotid arteries. But what would the point be? I love my wife and her goal was one that was beneficial. In light of that, it left me feeling ridiculous and/or ashamed to do anything other than eat healthier.

The same goes for my Christian walk. I need to follow God. I need to read my Bible daily. I need to memorize scripture. I need to share what I believe with others. And yet, I don't do all of those things consistently all of the time. Self-discipline and motivation falter when I am alone or feel like I am alone. When I have a partner or friend that can come beside me and remind me of those things, to challenge me in those things, my response will be automatic. Why? Because the closeness shared yields encouragement that a disciplined walk with Christ is not out of reach, but is actually attainable.

The Bible states the principle in Proverbs 27:17 as iron sharpening iron.[56] And how we need iron. We live in an age where society shouts from all corners that there are no absolutes, that truth is relative; and if truth really exists it doesn't count and isn't fair. Self-help books and counseling gurus claim that if we abstain from what the world enjoys, we are denying ourselves of innate needs and we will no doubt be weak because of it. In the privacy of our homes, we can turn on any computer or television and be inundated with offensive humor, pornography, and covetousness. Without another to come alongside of us to sharpen us and keep us true, we will find ourselves very alone in a battle that never ceases. And that is how the devil wants us. Alone. Then little by little the tempter seeks to wear down our defenses until we are dulled to the lies of the world and find ourselves partaking in death under the guise of enjoyment.

Two friends of mine—Melvin and David—serve as iron for me. We live in different cities, we have different jobs and yet when I speak with them, I know we are the same. We have the same goal— to glorify God and live a life that is worthy of bearing the name of Christ. At times I forget this goal; other times I remember it, but find myself weary in trying to attain it—and yet the mere sound of their voices strikes me and encourages me like a sharpening stone against the blade.

Through their friendship, I find the blessed abrasiveness that scrapes off reluctance and selfishness and sinfulness. No longer alone letting the worldly residue build up on my defenses, I feel renewed and challenged by each talk about Christ and about his plans for us. It is a true joy to talk, to be with, and to dream with these two—they are my iron.

As a believer, you need to find your "iron." Not only because it helps you stay accountable, but it also helps to keep others accountable. Even the strongest Christian needs to come up to his/her fellow believers and be iron—to sharpen himself/herself and to sharpen others. In days when you are weak, they will help you stand and before you know it, you will find that your walk is easier—not because it actually is an easy walk, but rather you are surrounded by encouragement and are stronger than before because of the friendly blows from iron that counteract the harsh blows of a world with nothing to offer.

washing clothes and
Brownie Points

When my wife and I were dating, we lived in two different cities. She lived in Oxford and I lived in Clinton. As a result, each
weekend one of us would jump in the car and drive off to the other
city and try to squeeze in as much time as possible with each other
before returning to our respective town and job. Due to our hectic
schedules, one of us would occasionally end up having to sit around
the house while the other would run errands. If I was stuck at her
house, I would play the guitar, read, and sometimes fold clothes.
I folded clothes because I knew Marni hated folding clothes, and
I figured I would get some extra points by folding clothes. While
folding clothes, I could just hear the conversations about how chiv-
alrous I was and how countless people should be envious of the
wonderful boyfriend that Marni had. Of course, I never heard any
such conversations, but the imaginary ones sufficed to boost my
pride and helped me continue folding clothes when I had a chance.

A year and a half after we started dating, we got married in
Oxford. After getting married, I found myself in a similar situation. My wife is the assistant girl's basketball coach at Oxford High
and soon she was at basketball practices, games, and tournaments,
which left me at home with spare time. Once again I started wash-
ing clothes and folding them and replaying conversations of the

various accolades that would (or at least should) be bestowed upon those who fold clothes without it being a requirement. I stopped short—is folding clothes now a requirement? If not, why isn't it a requirement now that I am married? And if so, well, that really stinks. I don't like to fold clothes—the only reason I did it before was to get "brownie points" and now that I am married, the points no longer exist. I was at home without anyone to witness my acts of servitude, except for our little dog and the fish in the aquarium. Now my servitude was up against the wall—whereas before my own pride, love for self-recognition, and enjoyment of personal accolades helped drive my folding of clothes, I was now left alone with simple, unglorified servitude that only exists out of a condition of the heart—that of being humble and considering others greater than oneself. Man, that really stinks. Then I found myself swamped with a rather bad attitude as I folded clothes—not my clothes, but *hers*. And I didn't enjoy it. I found that I had to pray and ask God for a new heart in the folding of clothes. It seemed so small, but it was something that I couldn't do without help. Not only that, but I had so long perpetuated my servitude through false humility that I found it hard to do anything with genuine humility. It isn't fun for the prideful to not only be humble, but to be humble and not have anyone notice that you were being humble.

This scenario plays itself out countless times from the beginning of God's choosing of his people to the present. People continually struggle a little when they find themselves doing similar things within a different paradigm. As a Christian, I discover things that were once "bonuses" now become requirements. As a result, the standard that I have to live up to is way above the worldly standard. This new paradigm of higher standards is seen through Jesus' earliest teachings in the Sermon on the Mount. He taught the people repetitively through a pattern of "you have heard it said.... I say..." I am sure the people in the crowd were both amazed by his wisdom and teachings and a little afraid of their ability to live up to these values. After Jesus came, the people could no longer be preoccupied about the act, but about the heart. For God's children to live in a godly fashion, Jesus taught that they must purge false piety and humility from among their ranks, and nothing purges these acts better than true acts of service.

For example, a non-Christian sees his neighbor, an elderly lady, trying to rake her leaves. He thinks, *Oh boy, I can do a good deed.* He walks over, helps rake her leaves, and walks away with both the elderly lady and himself thinking *Wow, what a nice guy.* The same neighbor a year later has become a Christian. Now when he sees the neighbor, not only does he see an elderly lady, but he also sees a way he can fulfill a commandment—take care of the fatherless and the widow. Love your neighbor as yourself. They will know us by the way we love each other. Now when he rakes her leaves, he goes with the intent not to serve himself, boost his self-image, or to help a lady, but to serve his God, glorify Him, and hopefully have others catch a glimpse of who his God is. No more walking away with the "what a nice guy" feeling. He must walk away with the "what a great God" feeling.

The bar is raised and there is no longer room for pride in acts of service. When the heart is not changed by God, this is a terrible, terrible thing. In fact, it can leave a person burned-out or cold of heart because giving without being refilled by God's love can leave one empty and hurt. But when the heart is changed, when there is that true sense of service and a sense that in every act of servitude we give God glory and honor—the reward is greater than any self-felicitating act ever can and will be.

snorkeling
or Hell

My brother, my father, and I went snorkeling. My mother went to Hell. My dad, brother, and I saw many types of tropical fish and a sunken ship. My mother took pictures of the landscape of Hell and sent our pastor a postcard from Hell's post office. Really.

We were in the Cayman Islands and since my mom didn't care to go snorkeling, she chose to go to Hell, Cayman Islands. It gets its namesake from the dark, mysterious geological formations and is a popular tourist spot. That day on our tour, we had two choices—go snorkeling or go to Hell. That was in 1989, and now I tell this story because of something that happened fifteen years later. I tell it in part to help explain in words what I failed to explain to my Chinese roommate, Shen, when we were talking about God.

My roommate was curious about church and went faithfully even though he didn't quite understand why we all went. He would ask questions, and we would often stay up for hours chatting about God and who we are in Christ. This was all very exciting, because Shen was "curious," which I knew meant God was tugging at his heart trying to get Shen to notice him.

One day he explained to me that he really didn't understand the Bible that well in English, so I told him I would find a video. I had a VCD from when I worked in China and dug it out from the mountain of clutter on my desk. I presented it to him and told him it presented the whole Bible story in about forty-five minutes of video snippets and animation.

He was interested in what he saw in the video, but one thing upset him and he couldn't focus on anything but this upsetting thought. At the end of the video, an animated clip shows Jesus sitting on the judgment seat, separating the people "as a shepherd separates the sheep from the goats." In fact, this video had a sequence of people in the background falling off a cliff into the abyss. It seemed a little overdone and the image of the animation stuck with Shen.

A day later in a department store, Shen brought up the video by asking, "Do you believe that there is a hell?" He followed it up with questions of "Does God send people there?" and "Why would he do that?" While trying to answer his questions, I failed to dispel his unsettled feeling towards the video and soon his curiosity diminished into a small ember burning with a cold, outward shell. Something I wanted him to know is that God didn't "make" those people go to Hell. God doesn't force people to Hell; he allows and wants them to come and live with him. There are only two choices—and everyone is going to Hell and the few that actually listen to God and heed his call to accept his all-sufficient gift of grace through his Son are the ones who are allowed into paradise.

We do not have an a) Hell b) Heaven or c) Other option despite all the world wants us to believe. Know that it was a human decision that broke the system and separated us from God. Know that God wants us to know him and see him. Know that God wants this so badly that he gave his only son. Know that it isn't his desire for us to go to Hell where we are eternally separated from him.

So the next time an unbeliever asks skeptically, "What kind of God sends people to Hell?" know you can answer that it must be a frightful one, but if they want to hear about a God who allows people to spend eternity in his presence, you know and love him and want to tell them all about him.

a history major's
Welding Skills

When I was in college, the last thing on my mind was what to major in; that is evident by how much I have used my actual major. I majored in history and since graduation I have worked as an assistant director of a Baptist Student Union, an emergency room secretary, a residence hall director, a conversational English teacher, and a high school ELL teacher. With the exception of a few games of *Trivial Pursuit* or watching an episode of *Jeopardy*, I haven't really put my knowledge of the antiquities to use.

My major and my lack of education in some fields is something that becomes even more highlighted in contrast to one of my latest adventures—welding. Well, actually, brazing—which means welding at lower temperatures. In theory, I wanted to braze things together because brazing torches ran at a lower temp and, therefore, might reduce the risk of my burning a limb off. In reality, any torch can burn you—as I found out when molten solder dripped onto my foot (I was wearing sandals, which lead me to believe the booklet that said wear "safety" clothing like boots and leather aprons).

I decided to use my new skill and try to build a bicycle. I started with old bicycles that I bought at a second-hand store, a reciprocating saw, a MAPP torch, and some brazing rods. I made my purchases without great haste—in fact, I drove by the old bikes twice before stopping, and I read all that Wikipedia had on the topics of brazing and welding. I think most people would agree that I was encroaching upon expert status. In fact, I thought if I started off with a bicycle, it would be easy to end up with a bicycle. It made sense and I set about this new adventure with my golden retriever-esqe optimism.

I cut the old bikes into pieces, laid the pieces next to each other and started torching away. If my goal was to torch things, I would have had great success right out of the blocks—but my intention was to braze pieces of pipe together. I could barely get the brazing rod to turn red, much less melt, which left me far from having metal pieces adhere to each other.

After reading a little further about the brazing process, I found out that I wasn't heating up the metals to a high enough temperature. I hadn't heated the metals to a high enough temperature because when the metal started turning red and/or white hot, I had started to get a little frightened of having something that hot near me and my bottle of flammable, pressurized gas. Soon I learned not to be a chicken about the heat, and I soon could heat things up until they would melt.

Despite my newfound skill of heating things up to extremely high temperatures, this still didn't help the brazing process like I thought it would. I could now melt the brazing rod and have the metals stick together, but the problem came after the metals had cooled down a bit. I could bump into my "brazed" metals and they would fall apart. I discovered this because I did bump into two of the pipes I had worked on and, upon falling to the ground, they broke apart. Needless to say, that was a little frustrating. I continued to try and try again with my brazing until I became so frustrated that I quit trying. I went on to build my bicycle out of a 2X6 piece of wood, a few 2X4s, PVC pipe, and nuts, bolts, and brackets. The bike I made actually worked well for a bike that weighed over 150 pounds, but it was a far cry from the visions of grandeur I had before starting the project.

A month or two later, my wife and I were having company

and we started cleaning up a little of the clutter that had collected through the house. One of the things I found while cleaning up was the instructions for my brazing torch. I kept it because it had a graph of which torches can actually braze metals, and I thought for sure my torch wasn't one of them. After cleaning a while, I dug out the pamphlet and started reading it. Nope, my torch can braze. Yep, it was my fault it didn't work. Yep, the instructions tell me how to do it right. Nope, I didn't read them the first time. The problem was not the heat, was not the torch, was not the brazing rods, and it was not the metals I was trying to braze together. The problem was that they were not clean. With a little chemistry knowledge, one finds that fire requires oxygen—that is a no-brainer. The problem was that metals undergo oxidation (which is what causes metals to rust) and with a layer of oxidized metal, the brazing rod would stick to it as opposed to the actual metal rod. The result was the equivalent of taking a Post-It note in sand and then trying to stick it on the wall. Just as the sand would get in the way of the Post-It note's ability to stick to the wall, the oxidized layer kept the metals from sticking together.

To remedy this problem, all it took was a trip to the local hardware store to buy a less-than-two-dollars-which-is-much-less-than-the-money-I-wasted wire brush. With this little, cheap, made-in-China, wire brush, I scrubbed the metal until it shined like a new quarter and brazing actually worked after that. Just like a business will frame its first dollar, I kept the first two pieces of metal that I brazed together. I have pounded on them and dropped them and amazingly, they remain stuck together. And why do they remain stuck together? Because nothing was in the way when they were initially stuck together.

The same goes with disciplines in my life. I am called to be holy as my father in Heaven is holy.[57] That definitely isn't going to stick if there is even a little of me in the way when I try. God commands us to do many things, but he doesn't send us unprepared. He seeks to equip us and we find that God is faithful and just to bring to completion the work that he began in us.[58] The statement to be holy[59]–and some translations state this verse as "be perfect"—always seemed out of reach. This is because I sought to have this command "stuck" to me, but I never was completely clean of what the world and my own nature brought to the amalgamation. As a result, the command never stuck and even the slightest bump sent me and the command scattering in different directions.

Through my failures, this command seemed impossible and as a result I eventually quit striving for it because I believed it was unrealistic and unattainable. In reality I was both right and wrong in saying that it was impossible. It is an impossible task if I try it on my own. If I try to be perfect with imperfect abilities and imperfect motives, I will surely fail. My own corrosion of self prevents this command and all of the others from sticking because the application of the principle began with my own effort. But if I try to be perfect and holy with God's help, then it is possible. If I begin by truly emptying myself and letting God be the beginning of my following—to deny myself, take up my cross, and then follow—then what was unattainable is now the only natural outcome.

The Bible states that with man it is impossible, but with God, all things are possible. I believe that God would not command us to do something that he knew we couldn't achieve. If that were the case, we would soon be trying to claim that many things were impossible like loving our enemies or laying down our lives for others. The command was to be perfect and the command stands because it is achievable through Christ, and we are not to relent until we achieve it.

May you find amongst your failures in following God a point where he can take you, strip you of yourself, and fill you up with his love, grace, and mercy—and then and only then will you find that his commandments are not impossible, but naturally possible.

Endnotes

1 Matthew 11:30

2 Mark 6:8

3 Psalm 46:10

4 Matthew 6:33

5 Hebrews 12:1

6 Hebrews 4:16

7 Hebrews 4:14–16

8 Psalm 4:3, 17:6, 18:6

9 Philippians 1:6

10 John 14:6

11 Matthew 5:12

12 Matthew 5:23–24

13 Matthew 19:14–"But Jesus said, 'Let the children alone, and do not hinder them from coming to Me; for the kingdom of heaven belongs to such as these.'"

14 Luke 7:47

15 Matthew 12:13

16 Matthew 8; Luke 7

17 Psalm 139

18 Matthew 23:25–26

19 1 Samuel 16:7

20 Matthew 9:36

21 Matthew 8:3 and Mathew 8:15

22 Matthew 9:25

23 Matthew 14:31

24 Matthew 19:13–15

25 Mark 10:15

26 1 Corinthians 10:13

27 1 Timothy 6:3–21

28 Read about these cool stories in the Gospels–The healing of Peter's mother-in-law (Matthew 8); Feeding of the 5,000 (Mark 6); Peter walking on the water (Matthew 14); The woman caught in adultery (John 8); Jesus reassuring Peter (John 21).

29 awe. (n.d.). Dictionary.com Unabridged (v 1.1). Retrieved June 08, 2007, from Dictionary.com website: http://dictionary.reference.com/browse/awe

30 Psalms 22:23–"You who fear the LORD, praise Him; All you descendants of Jacob, glorifying Him, And stand in awe of Him, all you descendants of Israel."

    Psalms 33:8–"Let all the earth fear the LORD; Let all the inhabitants of the world stand in awe of Him."

    Psalms 65:8–"They who dwell in the ends of the earth stand in awe of Your signs; You make the dawn and the sunset shout for joy."

31 Acts 2:43

32 Hebrews 12:28

33 Luke 19:41

34 Matthew 9:13, 12:7

35 Matthew 20:34

36 Ezekiel 36:25–27

37 Hebrews 12:1–"Therefore, since we have so great a cloud of witnesses surrounding us, let us lay aside every encumbrance and the sin which

so easily entangles us, and let us run with endurance the race that is set before us."

38 1 Corinthians 9:24–"Do you not know that those who run a race all run, but *only* one receives the prize? Run in such a way that you may win."

39 2 Timothy 2:5–"Also if anyone competes as an athlete, he does not win the prize unless he competes according to the rules."

40 Matthew 22:34–40

41 Psalm 27:13

42 Matthew 18:21

43 Matthew 6:14–15

44 Matthew 6:10–13

45 Romans 10:14 "How then will they call on Him in whom they have not believed? How will they believe in Him whom they have not heard? And how will they hear without a preacher?"

46 1 John 1:3 "what we have seen and heard we proclaim to you also, so that you too may have fellowship with us; and indeed our fellowship is with the Father, and with His Son Jesus Christ."

47 Philemon 1:6–"and I pray that the fellowship of your faith may become effective through the knowledge of every good thing which is in you for Christ's sake."

48 Luke 7:37–story of the "sinful woman" anointing Jesus' feet. The name "sinful woman" is not found in the scriptures, but rather as a heading in NIV Bibles.

49 Matthew 23:3 "therefore all that they tell you, do and observe, but do not do according to their deeds; for they say things and do not do them."

50 1 Corinthians 8:9–13

51 1 Corinthians 9:1

52 If anyone supposes that he knows anything, he has not yet known as he ought to know; but if anyone loves God, he is known by Him. Therefore concerning the eating of things sacrificed to idols, we know

that there is no such thing as an idol in the world, and that there is no God but one. For even if there are so-called gods whether in heaven or on earth, as indeed there are many gods and many lords, yet for us there is *but* one God, the Father, from whom are all things, and we *exist* through Him.

53 Matthew 23:25–"Woe to you, scribes and Pharisees, hypocrites! For you clean the outside of the cup and of the dish, but inside they are full of robbery and self-indulgence."

54 1 Samuel 16:7–"But the LORD said to Samuel, 'Do not look at his appearance or at the height of his stature, because I have rejected him; for God sees not as a man sees, for man looks at the outward appearance, but the LORD looks at the heart.'"

55 James 1:7–"Do they not blaspheme the fair name by which you have been called?"

56 Proverbs 27:17–"Iron sharpens iron, so one man sharpens another."

57 1 Peter 1:15–"But just as he who called you is holy, so be holy in all you do; for it is written: "Be holy, because I am holy.""

58 Philippians 1:6–"For I am confident of this very thing, that He who began a good work in you will perfect it until the day of Christ Jesus."

59 Matthew 5:48–"Therefore you are to be perfect, as your heavenly Father is perfect."